BRIDGING THE LEARNING/ ASSESSMENT GAP

Showcase Teaching

Wayne Jennings
Joan Caulfield

ScarecrowEducation
Lanham, Maryland • Toronto • Oxford
2005

Published in the United States of America
by ScarecrowEducation
An imprint of The Rowman & Littlefield Publishing Group, Inc.
4501 Forbes Boulevard, Suite 200, Lanham, Maryland 20706
www.scarecroweducation.com

PO Box 317
Oxford
OX2 9RU, UK

British Library Cataloguing in Publication Information Available

Library of Congress Cataloging-in-Publication Data
Jennings, Wayne, 1930–
  Bridging the learning/assessment gap : showcase teaching / Wayne
Jennings, Joan Caulfield.
    p. cm.
  Includes bibliographical references and index.
  ISBN 1-57886-194-2 (pbk. : alk. paper)
  1. Teaching. 2. Learning, Psychology of. 3. Learning—Physiological
aspects. 4. Brain. I. Caulfield, Joan, 1940– II. Title.

LB1025.3.J44 2005
370.15'23—dc22

                                        2004018831

CONTENTS

FIGURES

INTRODUCTION

In this book, we offer the reader powerful brain-compatible and research-based teaching and learning strategies based on how the brain works. This format presents educators with a useful framework for understanding how to design instruction. It will help answer questions about why some approaches to teaching are more successful than others with students.

We will not get mired in the physiology of the brain, as we do not find it necessary to have an exhaustive knowledge of its structures in order to be a successful teacher. Instead, we emphasize a broad outline of general knowledge of those processes that affect school practice. We showcase teaching strategies that align with the brain's natural functioning.

Continuing dramatic developments in the ability of neuroscientists to look inside the brain to discover its incredible intricacy place awesome responsibility on all of us to optimize learning for the young people who cross the thresholds of our classrooms. The need is urgent; the research is available.

There has never been a shortage of innovations in American education. They come, they stay, and then they are conquered by another solution! They resurface with some tweaking of the name and become supposedly something new and different. Think of the Socratic seminar.

It seems that schools are always reconfiguring, revamping, and reconsidering priorities to respond to the "latest." The educational ditches are littered with innovations because decision makers are generally not grounded in a strong foundation that provides a lens to examine whether the "latest" is the "best."

Debates have raged for decades over whether teaching is an art or a science. Those who believe it is an art argue that great teachers are born, not made; others believe that by providing dedicated teachers with sound pedagogy, teachers will transform into greatness. Of course, teaching is both art and science. What is that science, that pedagogy of learning? That's the subject of this book.

Complicating the challenge of teaching is the changing face of the United States because we must succeed at the unmet goal of educating all Americans: African, Asian, Caucasian, Latino, and Native American. Twenty percent of American students have at least one foreign-born parent. Almost 10 million kids speak a language other than English at home, two-thirds of them speaking Spanish. Astoundingly, 52 percent of preschool-aged children are now in school compared to only 21 percent in 1970 (Publication Education Network, 2003). Achievement gaps between Black and Latino students and Caucasian students are shameful and unacceptable.

Our children lead much more complicated, plugged-in lives. We know that more and more is expected from schools every year. Today, the teacher has many roles: instructor, facilitator, guide, friend, coach, and counselor. We agree that no longer can we just teach the 3 Rs. In fact, some would argue that the 3 Ts are equally important: teamwork, thinking skills, and technology.

In spite of these challenges, we must seek ways to continuously improve instructional delivery. Stakeholders are serious about No Child Left Behind (NCLB). For the foreseeable future, the reality is that regardless of who is in power in Washington, school accountability and the requirement that all children will learn mean some iteration of NCLB will shape American educational practice.

In addition to numerous books about the brain, four additional seminal areas of work reinforce the progress of educational practices related to brain-compatible learning.

- One of these is that of learning styles research, which advocates claim are biologically based cognitive tendencies or preferences. Among those developing models about learning styles are Anthony Gregorc (1985), Rita and Kenneth Dunn (Dunn & Dunn, 1993), and Bernice McCarthy (2000). They assert that people differ in their responses to learning conditions because of inbred personal preferences. For example, the Dunns list some 21 preferences ranging from such areas as amount of light, room temperature, types of seating, working alone or with others, time of day, degree of responsibility, and impulsivity.
- A second field is the work in the area of multiple intelligences (Gardner, 1983). Although there is little actual research on the theory of multiple intelligences, the broad acceptance and common-sense experience of educators make it a viable concept.

Clearly, these two fields address human variability. We cite two other distinguished sources and their recommendation as to how learning occurs:

- One of these is the American Psychological Association, which has published *Learner-Centered Psychological Principles: A Framework for School Redesign and Reform* (1997) based on considered opinions and research by a broad-based panel of distinguished scholars.
- A second is the work from the National Research Council (2000), which has published *How People Learn: Brain, Mind, Experience, and School*, also a work by a distinguished panel of scholars from many fields.

These four authoritative sources of information about learning constitute the bedrock foundation for this book and for the modern educator who wishes to work successfully with the brain.

Brain-compatible education is not a fad or another experiment in education. It holds the promise of genuine reform based on valid research. Our advice: Become critical consumers of the application of brain research for the classroom. Educators need to read, discuss, and provide quality staff development in order to combine new knowledge with the vast wealth of experiential wisdom that has been amassed during years of teaching. Neuroscience is providing useful strategic insights about new ways to work with our students.

Still, we must separate pseudoscience from real science and not jump to conclusions based upon exaggerations and fabrications. Remember how easily and quickly the work of Roger Sperry in the 1960s on right-brain/left-brain theory was popularized. Students were labeled right-brained or left-brained as though it was all right for Johnny not to read because he was an artistic child who was right-brained. Students so labeled are denied other venues for learning. Of course, we now better understand that we are whole-brained unless the corpus callosum that divides the two hemispheres has been severed, as confirmed by Sperry's research. His contribution helped us understand how brain areas are specialized. We also understand the limitations of left-right brain diagnosis.

It is a new and different world in education for all of us, no matter our age. The public school is no longer considered the only route through which children can experience equity and access to the riches of schooling. Many consider the boom of student population in private, parochial, charter, and homeschooling a threat. Others seize the opportunity to examine their understanding of best knowledge and best practice. It will be essential to understand the best that is known about learning and use that knowledge to make schooling more effective. What is unique today is that knowledge about the brain's functioning is at the highest level in history.

Is this discouraging? No, we must "Seize the day," as Robin Williams admonished his students to do in *Dead Poets Society*. The Chinese believe that with every danger, there is opportunity. We suggest that there is opportunity to reflect, revisit, retool, and react appropriately and meaningfully to new paradigms.

However, there is a huge problem. Each state has developed very specific standards and expectations for its students on one end; on the other end, very rigorous testing has been instituted. The missing link is the discovery of what instructional practices are effective in supporting teachers as they prepare their students for increased expectations.

This book is not intended to be all-inclusive with every possible strategy. It is intended as a springboard for beginning internal conversation about exciting, powerful learning experiences that teachers can use to incite learning in their classrooms. Like the signs you see—"Pardon Our Dust" or "Work In Progress"—this book will help you think in new ways about your "work in progress." At the least, some of these strategies will energize your teaching—give you a new zest and enthusiasm. At its best, this book can provide you with a chance to think flexibly, not just outside the box but well beyond it. Like all strategies, nothing is so unique that it has never been thought of before. However, there is always a new twist, a better mousetrap, if you will!

1

FOUNDATION FOR LEARNING

Neuroscientists peering inside the brain with new specialized imaging devices and discovering its incredible complexity have given us a splendid opportunity so that no child *is* left behind.

With neuroscientists using ever more sophisticated imaging, no longer must we depend on static pictures of the brain as in an x-ray; imaging devices now allow us to see the brain and its intricacies in real-time action. Scientists began with the PET scan (positron emission tomography). UCLA researcher Dr. Michael E. Phelps was one of the first to show in striking detail how different parts of the brain are activated when performing mental tasks such as hearing, reading, talking, and thinking. This invasive procedure allowed scientists to view the brain after radioactive glucose was injected into a vein. Because of the radioactivity, however, this could only be performed on a subject a limited number of times.

Then came the noninvasive fMRI (functional magnetic resonance imaging), which uses powerful magnets to generate detailed images of the brain's structure by identifying areas of the brain receiving large amounts of oxygen. Increased oxygen indicates active areas of thought and memory and allows scientists to identify where current brain functions are taking place.

The newest imaging device, called magneto-encephalography (MEG), allows scientists to analyze magnetic signals associated with electrical currents in the brain. This process may permit doctors to do amazing things like detect disorders such as cerebral palsy before a baby is born. As shown in Figure 1.1, PET, fMRI, and MEG imaging techniques open a window on that mysterious and remarkable three-pound organ, the brain.

Some critics argue that we do not know enough yet to bridge the gap between neuroscience and education. They believe that although the

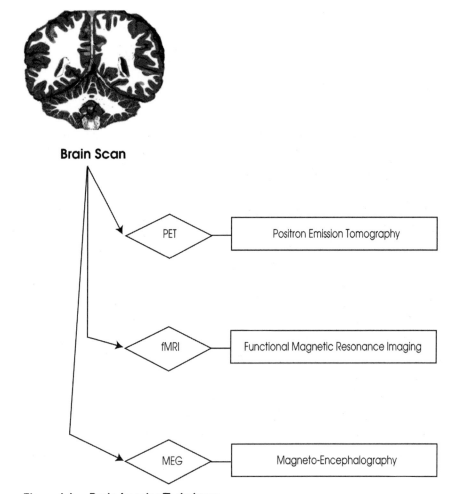

Figure 1.1. Brain-Imaging Techniques

research is promising, we are not really ready to apply it to the classroom. These critics argue that neuroscience has little to say to desperate educators seeking solutions to complex problems of instruction. In sum, they believe that in an effort to "do the right thing" we can fall prey to unfounded claims that a new strategy is proven by brain research.

Other voices believe that there is no time to waste. If research is available to support efforts to carry out the awesome responsibilities of preparing the minds of the students who cross the classroom thresholds every day, then we must use it. They point out that findings from neuroscience have been the impetus for developing promising new programs, such as the Fast ForWord software program from the Scientific Learning Corporation in which neuroscientists at Stanford University have used fMRI to observe brain activity of dyslexic children that are proving to help these children read almost normally in as little as 12 weeks by "rewiring or reprogramming" their brains (Temple, 2003).

What, then, are we learning from neuroscience that is of particular importance to teachers? There are scores of neuro- and cognitive scientists and interpreters who have published findings that have a direct impact on education—Howard Gardner from Harvard, Marian Diamond at the University of California at Berkeley, Joseph LeDoux at New York University, Antonio Damasio at the University of Iowa, Mihaly Csikszentmihalyi at the University of Chicago, Candace Pert at Georgetown University, Marcus Raichle at Washington University in St. Louis, Michael Phelps at UCLA, and Harry Chugani at Wayne State University, to name just a few.

Among respected interpreters of that research are Renate and Geoffrey Caine, Leslie Hart, Eric Jensen, Susan Kovalik, Robert Sylwester, Pat Wolfe, and the authors of this book. Their contributions provide a working knowledge of the applications of brain research for education. Figure 1.2 lists some of the well-known interpreters of brain research.

While there is much that remains a mystery about how exactly the brain works—for example, how quadrillions of instances of memory are stored—there is general agreement from neurologists and cognitive scientists about the brain and its role in learning. Most obvious, of course, is that the brain is the organ for learning. Obvious as this is, no one paid this much attention until the past two decades. Now, almost every conference and workshop has one or more sessions about the brain. The

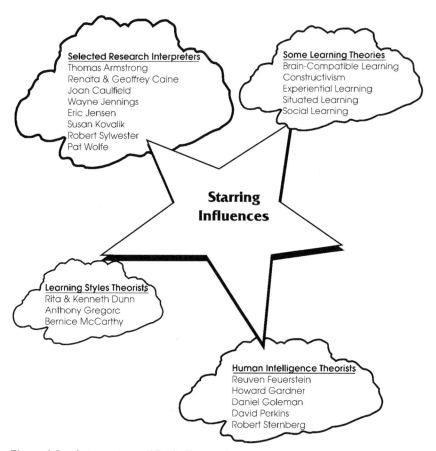

Figure 1.2.   Interpreters of Brain Research

specialized references at the end of this book lists many recent books about the brain's relationship to learning. What can be distilled from the research on the brain for learning? The following is a summary of the salient points of brain research and the implications for learning from interpreters.

EACH BRAIN IS AS UNIQUE AS A FINGERPRINT

Although the general architecture of the brain follows the same pattern among people, the details vary enormously. We all have neurons and dendrites, a neocortex and an amygdala, and the other basic structures of the human brain. From a physical standpoint, however, there are huge differences in the number of connections among neurons, differences in how well developed parts of the brain are, and differences in the speed of processing. Heredity impacts all of these, as does environment. Consider also that each of us experiences life uniquely; therefore, those experiences and memories that make up our learning will be infinitely varied and coded differently within our brains.

The functioning of the brain can be so totally different from other brains that it may be hard to comprehend. For example, though exceedingly rare, a few people have a photographic memory; some can recall every word of a book they've read, and some can mentally calculate difficult mathematical problems. On a more common level, there are clear and obvious differences in our brains—for example, when it comes to artistic and musical skills or ability to decode words on the printed page. Clearly, one-size instructional approaches or the exact same expectations for all students violate the nature of the human brain.

THE BRAIN CHANGES PHYSIOLOGICALLY AS A RESULT OF EXPERIENCE

The individual person's environment determines to a large extent the brain's functioning ability according to research done by Dr. Marian Diamond. She established the concept of neural plasticity, the brain's ability to change its structure and function in response to external experiences. It is startling (and reassuring to adults) that new brain connections can occur at any age. Diamond (1988) showed with laboratory rats the power of an enriched environment to increase brain growth.

The work of Michael Phelps and Harry Chugani with the PET visually depicts the brain's energy use and has opened the door to the study of the brain's operation at various ages (Phelps, 2003). Humans build neuronal connections called dendrites at the fastest rate from birth to about age 10. Growth slows considerably after age 10, and the number of connections slowly declines as we age. Chugani posits that not only does the child's peak learning occur during the years of the greatest dendrite growth, but that during those years, the brain has a remarkable ability to adapt and reorganize itself as well. Of course, these findings have profound importance for early childhood education. Another direct implication of this window of opportunity is the timing of second-language acquisition. Although language can be learned at any age, there is a greater chance of success and fluency if instruction begins early. Much recent research at the National Institute of Mental Health (2001) has focused on the teenage brain and its window of opportunity. The prefrontal cortex, which is responsible for planning, organization, and decision making, is not fully formed in the teenage brain. Around 9 or 10 years of age, the brain undergoes a growth spurt when neurons begin sprouting many new connections. At about 12 years of age, the brain begins a pruning process of eliminating those connections not being used. This allows the brain to work more efficiently. Clearly, the brain is not static. It is forever changing based on life's experiences.

IQ IS NOT FIXED AT BIRTH

Dr. Marian Diamond's work with laboratory rats and their environment was replicated with young children by Craig and Sharon Ramey, then at the University of Alabama (Ramey & Ramey, 1999). Their research proved that intervention programs could prevent children in impoverished environments from developing low IQs or retardation. This extremely valuable finding gives hope to the nation that instead of these children falling two years behind developmentally, their academic accomplishments can match peers from more favorable upbringing by providing early interventions.

INTELLIGENCE IS MULTIPLE

Howard Gardner states that human intelligence encompasses a far wider and more universal set of competencies than a single general intelligence reflected by an IQ score (Gardner, 1983). Working with a carefully crafted set of criteria, Gardner originally identified seven different intelligences (now eight) and allows that there is the possibility of more. The theory of multiple intelligences (MI) makes two important claims that are significant for educators: (1) All humans possess all the intelligences but in different strength configurations, and (2) Understanding and utilizing MI in the classroom opens the door for school success for students who don't learn well verbally-linguistically or logically-mathematically and for those who feel that the classroom is boring, disconnected, or too difficult. It is affirming to tell parents that their children are intelligent, albeit in different ways; and that teachers can help each student succeed in school. Adults embrace the validation that multiple-intelligence concepts offer, especially if they have felt like second-class students from their own school days.

LEARNING IS STRONGLY INFLUENCED BY EMOTION

Emotional Intelligence by Daniel Goleman (1995) and *The Emotional Brain* by Joseph LeDoux (1996) have advanced our understanding of the role of emotion in learning. Goleman's startling comment that emotional intelligence (EQ) is as important or more important than general intelligence (IQ) struck an immediate responsive note and his book became a best seller in the business and popular reading market.

The paramount importance of the emotional intelligence concept to society is such that school problems (unmistakably worse today than in former times) will never be solved or even mitigated to a significant degree without strongly focused efforts addressed to the emotional brains of students. Educators have observed that retention is strongest when the brain is accompanied by an emotion-laden experience, such as joy, thrill, satisfaction, laughter, and sadness. Students must genuinely feel respect by their teachers. However, short-term, quick-fix, feel-good solutions smack of manipulation, and the implications of these concepts mean far more than lip service or an approach of kindness. The impact of a rigid curriculum without attention to individual student needs says, "Your ideas and interests are not important here." While unspoken, in many schools that thought prevails as an unwritten background philosophy. The empowerment of students leads to greater engagement of the brain through an emotional kick. The clear message: Our emotional brains deserve the utmost respect and attention.

THE BRAIN NEEDS SECURITY

Most of the higher learning we aim for in schools is captured in the neo-cortex of the brain, an area sensitive to danger or anxiety. Under threat, the brain marshals its defenses, summons adrenaline, and in extreme cases prepares for fight or flight. Under such conditions, the brain's slower-acting neocortex largely shuts down and the student cannot tap the neocortex sufficiently when unduly anxious or feeling unsafe. Under extreme stress, clear thinking and even the power of speech may be temporarily lost.

Bad home situations—including those where children are "emotional orphans" or where they experience threats from bullies, sarcastic remarks, humiliation, fear, or embarrassment—all these and more may reduce the student's full brainpower for learning. These conditions may prevail in classrooms more than one would suppose. A fairly high percentage of students do not do well in highly academic settings and thus worry about low grades or failure and the attendant parental disappointment or cutting remarks from peers about being a "dummy." It's commonly thought that about 20 percent of students are high in Howard Gardner's multiple intelligences of verbal-linguistic and logical-mathematical skills that are the foundation for school success; this leaves 80 percent at stages of discomfort ranging from mild to severe.

For maximum learning in school, a relaxed, easy level of comfort serves the brain best. Students learn from challenges as long as the challenge is within their comfort level. This varies greatly among students in the kinds of challenges they will accept. Some feel very secure in themselves and their abilities. Some are greater risk takers, and some are more fearful, perhaps because of past traumatic experiences.

Leslie Hart, a pioneer in writing about the brain, proposed that threat caused the brain to, in effect, downshift from the cerebral cortex where higher-level thinking occurs to the limbic system or even to the brain stem where such primitive brain actions such as fight or flight reside. He based this on the early work of Dr. Paul MacLean, chief of the Laboratory of Brain Evolution and Behavior at the National Institute of Mental Health in Bethesda, Maryland (Hart, 1998). Newer research shows that our emotions and our limbic system are actually the driving force, the gatekeepers to our brain, through a small organ deep in the brain, the amygdala. Whether one calls the process "downshifting" or an override of rational thinking processes, the fact remains that threat impedes learning significantly.

THE BRAIN ENJOYS LEARNING

The young child constantly prowls and explores. Motivational programs are not necessary; we might say the child is driven to learn. We no more need to teach the child's brain to learn than we need to teach the stomach to extract nutrients. Clearly, the brain is made for learning. The clearest statement of this principle is from Frank Smith: "We underrate our brain and our intelligence . . . reluctance to learn cannot be attributed to the brain. Learning is the brain's primary function, its constant concern, and we become restless and frustrated if there is no learning to the done. We are all capable of huge and unsuspected learning accomplishments without effort" (Smith, 1988, p. 18).

These statements may not square with the experiences of many teachers who report widespread student disinterest in learning and a slow, labored pace of learning. The problem is that while the brain is an eager learner and is capable of rapid learning, it is also highly selective and does not attend well to topics that are not meaningful. Teachers struggle to motivate students to make a topic meaningful but this only works with student buy-in.

We have all observed how infants aggressively seek experiences. Their brains automatically strive to establish meaning. It is equally obvious how the brain is picky about what it accepts. Material that is too remote or difficult is rejected and not processed. Already-learned material runs the danger of boring the student—hence, the importance of a student-centered environment. The student, driven by an acquisitive, seeking brain, strives to understand and master the environment and to be seen as competent. Student brains differ one from another and teachers need a palette of strategies in order to tailor instruction.

THE BRAIN REQUIRES STIMULATION TO FLOURISH

We need to pay great attention to the critical factor of stimulation, meaning the brain's hunger for input. We may rightly consider the brain's need for input as insatiable. Consider it highly likely that the brain is starved for input in most classrooms much of the time. The brain forms connections from the flow of incoming data and one could say almost without fear of contradiction that the more input, the more learning. The brain thrives on input. Amazingly, contrary to how we might think, the input does not need to be highly organized and sequenced. The brain, an enormously powerful pattern-detecting device, sorts random input into patterns when provided large quantities of details, variations of situations, and ample opportunities to "play with" or manipulate the material.

One sees this most clearly in infants, who learn language and its structure without lessons or an articulated, sequenced curriculum. In fact, were adults to establish an infant curriculum for talking, the likelihood of the need to start tutoring or remedial talking programs would soon rear its expensive head. There are optimal environments for learning to talk. They consist of homes where, for example, there is talking with the youngster, reading to the youngster, asking the child to explain something, and adults talking among themselves in the presence of the child. These afford high input, stimulation, activity, and modeling. This illustrates the brain's extraordinary capacity for extracting meaning from the environment and organizing enormous streams of incoming data. As an example of a remarkable feat by the brain, consider how an infant in a bilingual home becomes fluent in two languages by age four without teachers, lessons, textbooks, work sheets, standardized tests, homework, and pain. This is astonishing given the difficulty of teaching foreign languages in schools. This kind of learning demonstrates the astounding capacity to store inconceivable numbers of patterns and programs in the child's brain.

THE BRAIN NEEDS NOVELTY AND CHALLENGE

The enemy of learning for the brain is a curriculum taught in the same way, day after day, class after class. While a stable environment and expected routines serve useful functions for the comfort of an individual, the brain enjoys new experiences, accepts challenges, and is intrigued by novelty. Teachers need to guard against a steady diet of textbook exercises unrelated to students' own questions. The classic comment by students about school and homework is that it is boring. We should pay heed; it signals a restless brain that has not found meaning or stimulation from the schoolwork. Again, infant learning serves as a model for all ages. Parents who talk to their children, take them places, and give them many new experiences to try their wings contribute greatly to the brain's development. The student for whom every day is the same will have a more limited development of the brain. Images of a brain at various ages prove that experiences dramatically increase the number of connections among neurons, the basic building blocks of the brain. Stimulation, novelty, and variety in the classroom grow brains and deepen learning.

THE BRAIN LEARNS BEST FROM CHOICE AND ACTION

An individual's brain is driven to test its learning and craves opportunities to invent and perform. The passivity of some classrooms deadens the brain's functioning. Students need to test their skills, be engaged, and participate. An inactive student probably means a brain in neutral; an active student means a brain in drive. Active does not necessarily mean physically active. It now appears that combining mental activity with physical activity yields faster and deeper learning.

One form of deeper brain engagement occurs almost automatically when choices are appropriately offered. The person's brain then must weigh the possible choices by thinking about their consequences and implications. Important choices generally entail considerable mental effort. In other words, the brain becomes engaged, which is what we as teachers want—active brains in our students! As an added bonus, offering choices reduces resistance to an imposed directive from the teacher, an unfortunate but natural human brain reaction.

THE BRAIN IS MEANING DRIVEN

The brain constantly seeks to understand, to see patterns, and to figure out situations. This works best when the brain can make connections or links to related experiences. Teachers understand this instinctively when they tell students the purpose of a lesson or how the topic relates to their lives. If a topic does not register as meaningful, the brain simply disengages and the teacher faces an uphill struggle. It is not sufficient to simply tell students that a topic is important. Students must feel or sense the meaningfulness in order to engage their brains.

This is a very subtle point. Schools introduce new material all the time. How can the brain be engaged if the new material doesn't meet the test of meaningfulness? We can resolve this by other aspects of the brain's functioning: novelty, excitement, and the skill of the teacher to provide a link to other learning or needs, such as the emotion of accomplishment. Skilled teachers will hook students on the topic with links to their brains' own drives for accomplishment, understanding, excitement, adventure, and status.

THE BRAIN SEEKS CONNECTIONS

From everything we know, the brain works by making connections among neurons, linking together similar information and memories. It would seem that the more connections, the more brainpower. Neurons that "fire together, wire together." What we know is captured in those connections and their complex interaction. These "patterns" in the brain become perfected over time with new experiences. The brain is unsurpassed as a pattern-detecting device. It superbly teases details from situations for what it needs to fill in and make corrections in its patterns.

Strangely, the brain learns more from complexity than from simplicity and from natural lifelike situations than artificial conditions. This is another tricky point for teachers who just naturally break down complexity into simplified basics—often a useful strategy, but strangely not generally brain compatible. The brain operates holistically; that is, it takes in the larger picture and fills in details later. Vice versa, it also uses details to create the big picture. It's a common experience for adults to hold a strong view but come to modify it as they become aware of details and other nuances. Hence, the more schools can be like life and use the world and its complex reality for learning, the greater the likelihood of success in reaching all students.

Teaching subjects separately in school runs the risk of making it harder for the brain to make connections. Subjects in schools are already divorced from real-world activities, thus limiting the brain's natural affinity to gain meaning from life. Interdisciplinary approaches solve some of this problem, as connections between the subjects are more apparent than when taught in isolation. This is because combining subjects makes for richer details and a more lifelike story. When we take a walk outside, we don't just see flowers separated from the rich context of their environment. We may focus on a flower; we may note the dry soil, the wind, and the weeds; a butterfly may come by; and other people may intrude on the scene. Our brains extract multiple meanings from a rich environment. Integrating subjects or teaching from a problem-based approach adds complexity that intrigues our brains and yields more learning.

THE BRAIN NEEDS FEEDBACK FOR GROWTH

The brain refines its basic building blocks of patterns and programs by receiving information as to their accuracy and efficiency.[1] The feedback may come as a result of the students themselves when they realize that they are off target in their intents, or it may come from others who offer suggestions or criticisms. Schools offer feedback by report cards and grades. Often, however, these are too general and remote in time from the actual work and therefore have a much more reduced impact. Students want to know how well they did, particularly if they feel competent at the task, but they want to know right away—the brain wants to know *immediately*—rather than days or weeks later. Most school feedback is too nonspecific to be of use to the brain. Feedback, whether in the form of suggestions or coaching, is most effective when delivered in a nonthreatening way, is closely related in time to the action, and is highly specific. Feedback is one of the most important factors to be aware of in creating showcase teaching.

Figure 1.3 provides a few of the salient points about the functioning of the brain.

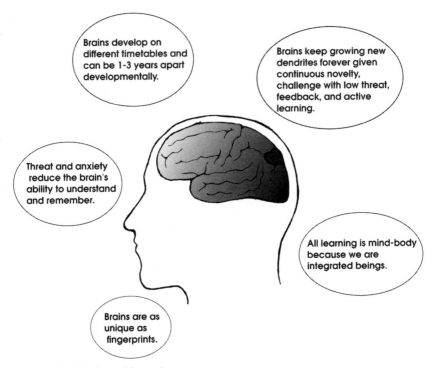

Figure 1.3. **Brain and Learning**

NOTE

1. Leslie Hart in *Human Brain and Human Learning* (1998) introduced patterns and programs as basic conceptual building blocks of the brain and brilliantly describes how these work. In general and highly simplified, patterns are the brain's understandings and programs are the brain's instructions.

2

FRAMEWORK FOR LEARNING

The No Child Left Behind legislation is leaving many of us feeling overwhelmed, scarred, and, at times, scared. It is not only children who are left behind in the new era of accountability. There are clear federal and state mandates that, if not met, have serious repercussions—all of this without adequate funding. School districts have responded by revising, mapping, aligning, and revamping their curricula to maximize the chance for all students to succeed. In this new climate, each must be reached—no excuses.

Now that we have mapped horizontally and vertically and aligned school district curriculum with state and national standards, what are the next steps? Can we now expect test scores that dazzle? Savvy educators know that well-written and well-honed curricula alone do not translate into student academic success. We all are acquainted with a curriculum that is gathering dust on a bookshelf. So what is the secret of having achievement that soars? We have always known that it is the teacher who is the magical catalyst who incites learning and ignites passion for learning.

True enough, there are teachers who seem to stumble into greatness. How much better for their colleagues, however, if they make instructional decisions based upon a well-reasoned philosophy of education and current pedagogy—the science of learning—that allows them to share and help others' teaching. We don't have all the answers, but we do know that neuroscience can and should inform our decisions. We don't want to rely only on what has worked for us in the past. To remain alive and engaged with our students, we need a wider palette of strategies that are brain compatible and research based. This can be the springboard for designing and creating powerful learning experiences for all students. The four basic principles of brain learning can be seen in Figure 2.1.

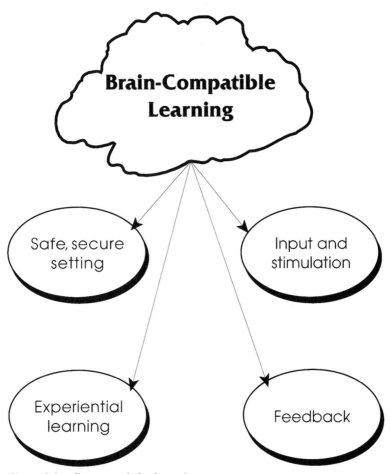

Figure 2.1.   Framework for Learning

A SAFE, SECURE SETTING

Tension, anxiety, and fear override the great thinking brain in all of us. Researchers have written on the impact of emotion and how it short-circuits thinking. The student must not be humiliated, demeaned, or shamed. There are many ways of ensuring the learner's comfort:

- Pay attention to the learner. We can greet the student on entrance and wish the student well at exit. When a learner returns from an absence, say, "Glad to see you back. We missed you. We were worried about you."

- Have a strong advisory program with daily contact and individual conferences. This accomplishes much more than the traditional homeroom period or the 300:1 student-counselor relationship. The advisor checks on the student every day and is available for consultation.

- Ask about the student's interests and adjust subject matter to accommodate burning questions. This conveys that students are important and their interests matter. The opposite position, of ignoring student interests and treating student brains as vessels to fill, demeans learners and results in all kinds of resistance, resignation, and apprehension, particularly at secondary school levels.

- Set a humane environment with attention to color, plants, decor, and work conditions. We all respond positively to attractive, convivial surroundings with interesting posters and comfortable furniture. The brain opens more to new information if comfortable and not threatened.

- Help fellow learners to know each other. A warm, supportive room of friends puts people at ease. Students working together on committees or teams come to understand each other and appreciate differences.

- Modify grading practices and systems to avoid sorting students into winners and losers. If you can't abolish the standard report card, at least provide a more complete picture of the student through samples of his or her work, portfolios, narrative reports, checklists, and conferences.

INPUT AND A RICH, STIMULATING ENVIRONMENT

Deprived of stimulation, the brain doesn't develop and, in fact, atrophies. We must immerse students in new material, real events, and projects, and use the world as the classroom. There are many ways to increase input to the brain:

- Increase the number of field trips and studies of the community. Schools will reallocate more for this area when they recognize its vital importance for learning. Even with limited budgets, teachers can make walking tours and study the community within a short distance of the school. The brain thrives on reality and complexity.
- Call upon the boundless resources of the community. Parents and other community members are a gold mine of skills and information. Many schools ask parents what they can share in such areas as travel experiences, places they have lived, careers, hobbies, health issues, politics, homemaking skills, and gardening. After cataloguing, staff have an enormous, free menu of resources.
- Offer a greater range of clubs and exploratory activities within the school day. This exposes students to interest areas, augments vocabulary, and may lead to talent development.
- Capitalize on the inherent differences within the student body. All schools have diverse populations. Rather than ignoring differences or treating diverse cultures as a problem, prize and benefit from differences and cultural contributions. Recognize different learning styles, personality types, and multiple intelligences. Make study of the diverse cultures and ethnic groups a part of the curriculum.
- Obvious as it is, use many approaches to learning. Draw upon manipulatives, displays, posters, visual media, experiments, models, sound, demonstrations, newspapers, periodicals, and technology.

MEANINGFUL, EXPERIENTIAL LEARNING

The brain compels students to try their skills and to become competent at tasks. Students must be active in school. The disjuncture between the energy of students and the passivity demanded by most schooling creates tremendous conflict. Students are like fast race cars gunning their engines at the starting gate—but the flag never falls. There are many ways schools have boosted active learning:

- Arrange exchanges with other schools. The exchange might be the school across town or in the next county or on another continent. It could be a virtual visit on the Internet. Exchanges require students to write letters, research destinations, prepare presentations and questions, and subject themselves to extraordinary real-life tests.
- Use project-based learning. Many conventional topics can be reformatted into challenges and searches for information to answer important questions. This technique is more powerful if students have shared in preparing questions based on their curiosity. Energy and motivation soar under conditions of participatory classroom democracy.
- Create teams to investigate topics. When students learn to work well together to solve problems or to propose answers to issues, their brains are more fully engaged in complex tasks. This better prepares students for the world of work and citizenship. Much has been written on the power of cooperative learning groups for increased learning and social growth.
- Active learning takes many forms: students teaching or tutoring others, internships, work experiences, cross-age activities, tour guides, video productions, mentoring experiences, producing newsletters for the school, drama productions, multimedia presentations, contests, solving school and community problems, and participation in governance. Teachers using these approaches report much greater enthusiasm, energy, and creativity with learners.

ACCURATE, TIMELY FEEDBACK

We most assuredly need timely and pinpointed feedback to help the brain develop more accurate knowledge. There are many ways of providing feedback beyond the usual report cards used to convey student achievement:

- Coaching at its best conveys the idea of gentle suggestions for improvement. People respond to kindly comments meant to help them understand the impact of their actions.
- Self-assessment and peer assessment provide feedback. Assessing results requires a high level of thinking and reflection about how well (or not so well) something turned out.
- Work samples and portfolios show what students have accomplished. Collected over time, student work can be compared with earlier work to show progress.
- Personal conferences with students provide one-on-one guidance. Conducted with utmost care and concern, teachers give students opportunities to reflect on their progress.
- Personal learning plans, discussed more fully in chapter 4, individualize education. Personal learning plans enable goal setting and provide a framework that guides students toward routes for accomplishing goals. They organize opportunities to review progress periodically.
- Teachers can make their objectives explicit. Students who clearly understand what is to be learned can better gauge their progress and adjust what needs to be accomplished.
- Software programs give instant feedback in a nonthreatening manner. Programs tailored to student needs can be endlessly patient with the student and allow for great differences in learning speed.
- Celebrations reinforce learning and highlight what was prized. Take time for fun and to recognize achievement. Special events arouse the emotions that energize student interest and excitement about content and skills.

In this book we will touch briefly on methods like cooperative learning, Socratic seminar, project-based/problem-based learning, and differentiated instruction as they relate to strategies. Each of these methods continues to command full texts. Methods are broad-based approaches and encompass many strategies. Our emphasis is on strategies that are specific instructional activities designed to enhance learning.

Breaking Ranks II: Strategies for Leading High School Reform (2004) by the National Association of Secondary School Principals offers seven "cornerstone" comprehensive strategies for schoolwide reform and improved student performance:

1. Establish the essential learnings a student is required to master in order to graduate, and adjust the curriculum and teaching strategies to help the student realize that goal.
2. Increase the quantity and improve the quality of interactions between students, teachers, and other school personnel by reducing the number of students for which any adult or group of adults is responsible.
3. Implement a comprehensive advisory program that ensures that each student has frequent and meaningful opportunities to plan and assess his or her academic and social progress with a faculty member.
4. Ensure that teachers use a variety of instructional strategies and assessments to accommodate individual learning styles.
5. Implement schedules flexible enough to accommodate teaching strategies consistent with the ways students learn most effectively and that allow for effective teacher teaming and lesson planning.
6. Institute structural leadership changes that allow for meaningful involvement in decision making by students, teachers, family members, and the community and that support effective communication with these groups.
7. Align the schoolwide comprehensive, ongoing professional development program and the individual personal learning plans of staff members with the content knowledge and instructional strategies required to prepare students for graduation.

Our strategies augment and make specific the broad-based methods of this important report, particularly number 4 of *Breaking Ranks II*. Our strategies are addressed to the teacher who must each day provide the spark for learning that actualizes school reform. We are confident that our strategies are teacher friendly and really define the term *school reform.*

What we are offering is a menu of exciting strategies that have the potential to energize your teaching and provide the novelty and stimulation that the brain craves. Several points beg for attention:

- We offer a limited menu of strategies, not exhaustive, or better said, exhausting! We have selected our top strategies for your

consideration. Are there more? Yes, scores of them—only con-
strained by imagination. We wanted to keep this book a perfect
size for study groups.

- These strategies can work with modification in any discipline from
physical education to advanced placement English.
- These strategies can excite students, support instructional goals,
and, in some cases, allow the teacher some flexible time with tar-
geted groups.
- Just because they are fun, novel, and engaging does not mean that
they are not powerfully effective.
- You will enjoy thinking of ways to make the strategy your own—to
give it your special twist. You may have the "better mousetrap."

Based on what is known about how students learn, teachers can check
their understanding, rationale, and strategies against a proposed framework
by asking the listed questions. As you look through each strategy, see if you
know why it is brain compatible based upon what we know about how students learn. Ask yourself the following questions about each strategy:

- Is there emphasis on context and meaning?
- Is there appropriate emotional impact?
- Are the eight intelligences served?
- Is there learning that occurs at a nonconscious level?
- Is there a body-brain connection?
- Is there low anxiety?
- Does the learning activity provide for enjoyment?
- Is there immediate feedback?
- Does it provide novelty?

New mandates require that instruction be scientifically based. The
federal law, No Child Left Behind, and the National Research Council
define scientifically based instruction. Figure 2.2 contrasts key points
from No Child Left Behind's requirement for "scientifically based" research and views from the National Research Council.

In chapters 3 and 4 we present teaching and learning strategies that
meet the criteria of scientifically based. Figure 2.3 summarizes a few of
the points we have made about how our brains work.

No Child Left Behind Act

1. Uses systematic methods that draw on observation or experiment.

2. Involves rigorous analyses to test hypotheses and justify conclusions.

3. Provides reliable and valid data across evaluators, observers, and studies.

4. Is evaluated using experimental designs.

5. Ensures that experimental studies are presented to allow for replication.

6. Has been accepted by a peer-reviewed journal or approved by a panel of independent experts.

Scientifically Based Research

National Research Council

1. Poses significant questions that can be investigated through observation.

2. Links research to relevant theory.

3. Uses a variety of methodological approaches.

4. Provides a coherent and explicit chain of reasoning.

5. Replicates and generalizes across studies.

6. Discloses research to encourage scrutiny and critique.

Figure 2.2.   Scientifically Based Research
Extrapolated from ASCD publication *INFOBRIEF:* August 2003

Brain Facts

Emotions impact learning. They deepen learning if appropriate in intensity.

The brain learns best if material is meaningful and linked to prior learning rather than factoids and isolated bits of information.

Each person's brain is unique and learns on its own timetable, with its own learning style and particular intelligences.

Active learning, hands-on learning, and project-based/ problem-based learning are ways of expressing the brain's preferencce for real, contextual-based learning experiences.

Figure 2.3.   Brain Facts

3

TEACHING STRATEGIES

In this chapter, we have carefully selected what we consider to be energizing strategies to begin an exciting instructional journey for you and your students. These suggestions are just a sample of the universe of teaching strategies, ones we consider appropriate for middle school, high school, and college, and are not presented or prioritized in any particular order. Each can be adapted, amplified, modified, or reduced to fit your style and situation. At the end of each strategy, we pose a few questions about its brain compatibility and provide sources for more information.

GRAPHIC ORGANIZERS

Graphic organizers provide ways for students to express their ideas and to promote critical thinking skills. Graphic organizers take many forms, as can be seen from the examples and from cited references. All stages of learning can benefit from the use of graphic organizers, from concept development to presentations.

Graphic organizers can be presented conceptually, hierarchically, sequentially, and cyclically. For example, sequential organizers can be

used for timelines (e.g., history), ages (e.g., child development), de-
grees of something (e.g., weight), or rating scales (e.g., achievement
in school); a cyclical organizer shows how events work together to
predict repeated results, such as the balance of nature or a cycle of
economic changes.

Software programs such as Inspiration allow easy creation and editing by individual students or with group projects. The following examples are a scant representation of the many forms this useful strategy
takes.

Examples of Graphic Organizers

The following examples (as seen in Figures 3.1 to 3.7) have been created and used by Amy Reilly and Jo McFadden, secondary school teachers in Hutchinson, Kansas.

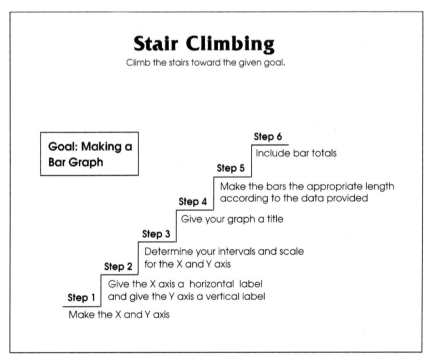

Figure 3.1.   Graphic Organizer: Stair Climbing

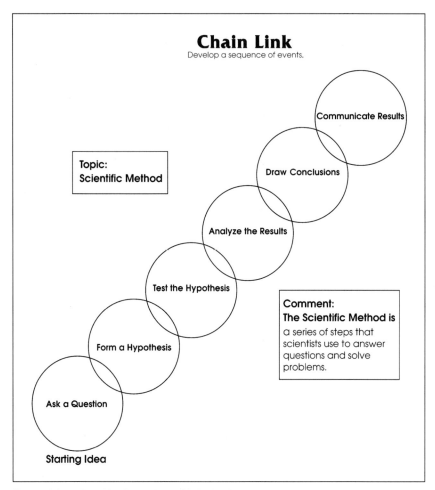

Chain Link
Develop a sequence of events.

Communicate Results

Topic:
Scientific Method

Draw Conclusions

Analyze the Results

Test the Hypothesis

Comment:
The Scientific Method is
a series of steps that
scientists use to answer
questions and solve
problems.

Form a Hypothesis

Ask a Question

Starting Idea

Figure 3.2.   Graphic Organizer: Chain Link

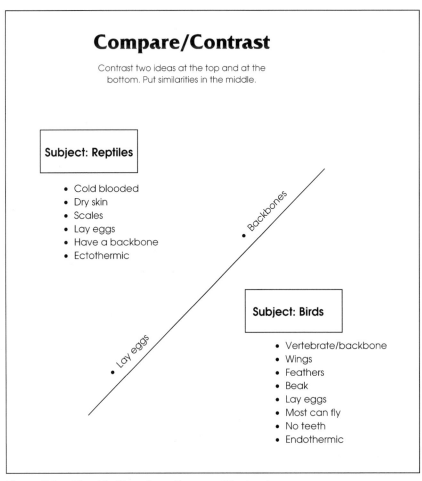

Compare/Contrast

Contrast two ideas at the top and at the bottom. Put similarities in the middle.

Subject: Reptiles

- Cold blooded
- Dry skin
- Scales
- Lay eggs
- Have a backbone
- Ectothermic

• Backbones

• Lay eggs

Subject: Birds

- Vertebrate/backbone
- Wings
- Feathers
- Beak
- Lay eggs
- Most can fly
- No teeth
- Endothermic

Figure 3.3. Graphic Organizer: Compare/Contrast

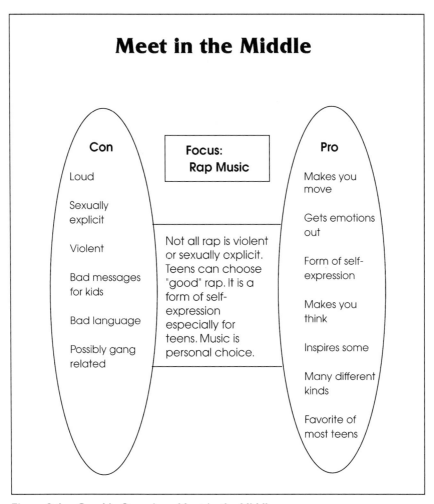

Meet in the Middle

Con

Loud

Sexually explicit

Violent

Bad messages for kids

Bad language

Possibly gang related

Focus: Rap Music

Not all rap is violent or sexually explicit. Teens can choose "good" rap. It is a form of self-expression especially for teens. Music is personal choice.

Pro

Makes you move

Gets emotions out

Form of self-expression

Makes you think

Inspires some

Many different kinds

Favorite of most teens

Figure 3.4.   Graphic Organizer: Meet in the Middle

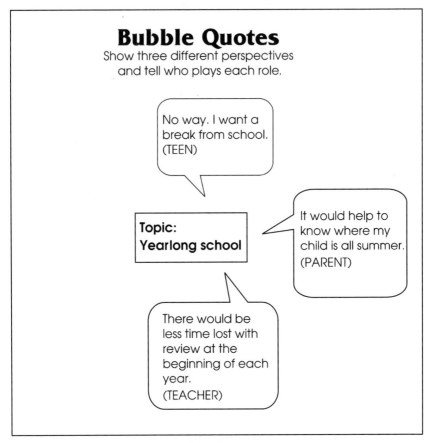

Figure 3.5.   Graphic Organizer: Bubble Quotes

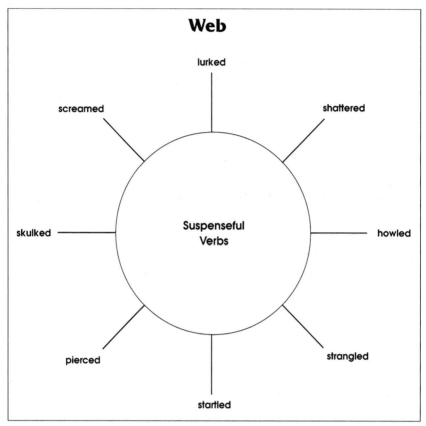

Figure 3.6.   Graphic Organizer: Web

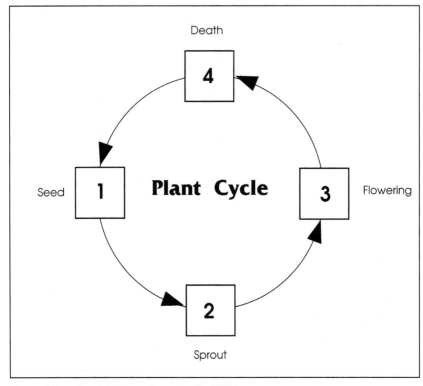

Figure 3.7.   Graphic Organizer: Cyclical Web

The graphic organizer in Figure 3.8 is a concept map developed by a team of teachers at Marcy School (Minneapolis, Minnesota) to plan an environmental studies unit that included planning, implementing, and evaluating an extended winter camping experience.

Why Use Graphic Organizers?

Graphic organizers help students integrate prior knowledge with new learning and see relationships between concepts (Dunston, 1992). They provide varied aspects of visual learning to meet differences in learning styles and multiple intelligences.

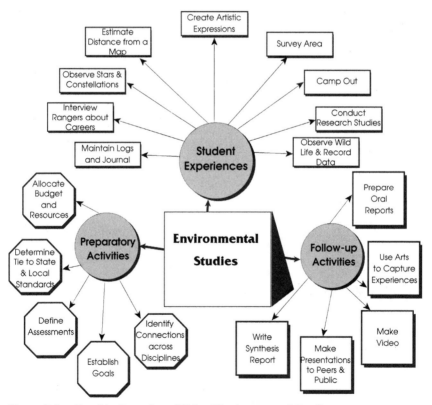

Figure 3.8.   Graphic Organizer: Web of Environmental Studies

Where Would a Teacher Use a Graphic Organizer?

- To focus attention
- To organize complexity
- To enhance concept understanding
- To introduce a new unit or topic
- To prepare for prewriting
- To connect seemingly disparate facts and information

How Does a Teacher Use a Graphic Organizer?

- Provide a graphic organizer template for students to complete.
- Have students create their own graphic organizer to demonstrate learnings.
- Use appropriate software to create mind maps and graphic organizers.

Brain Compatibility: Do You Agree?

Is there emphasis on context and meaning?	Yes	No
Are the multiple intelligences awakened?	Yes	No
Is there low stress and high enjoyment?	Yes	No
Is there immediate feedback?	Yes	No
Is there active involvement?	Yes	No
Does it provide novelty?	Yes	No

For More Information

- www.ncrel.org/sdrs/areas/issues/students/learning/lr2refer.htm
- *Brain-Compatible Classrooms* by Robin Fogarty
- www.teach-nology.com/web_tools/graphic_org/
- www.graphic.org/links.html

CHALK TALKS

Chalk talks are a silent way to reflect, generate ideas, check on learning, develop projects, and solve problems. With the ideas expressed by students, chalk talks may take on the form of a graphic organizer or concept map, as seen in Figure 3.9.

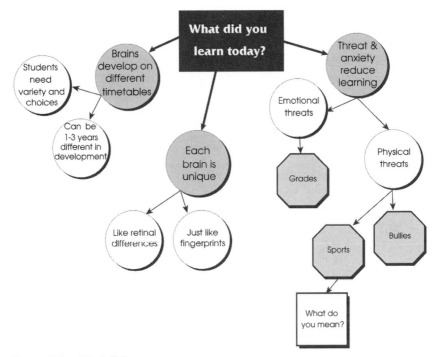

Figure 3.9.   Chalk Talks

Examples of Chalk Talks Topics

- What did you learn today?
- So what? Or, Now what?
- What do you know about . . . ?
- Next steps?

Why Use Chalk Talks?

Chalk talks deepen student understanding of concepts and relationships.

Where Would a Teacher Use Chalk Talks?

Chalk talks can be used before beginning a unit or at the culmination of a unit as a way to determine student learning and depth of understanding.

How Does a Teacher Use Chalk Talks?

- Teacher places pieces of chalk or markers at the board.
- Teacher writes a relevant question on the board.
- Teacher invites four or five students to the board, gives each a piece of chalk, invites students one at a time (but as students feel moved) to write a response to the question or to comment with a chalk remark on other responses or connect ideas with a line or to add question marks.
- When the students at the board have exhausted their ideas, they may hand off the chalk to another student who wishes to add, clarify, or question a response.
- The teacher may participate with students particularly to keep the chalk talk productive.

Brain Compatibility: Do You Agree?

Is there emphasis on context and meaning?	Yes	No
Are the multiple intelligences awakened?	Yes	No
Is there low stress and high enjoyment?	Yes	No
Is there immediate feedback?	Yes	No
Is there active involvement?	Yes	No
Does it provide novelty?	Yes	No

For More Information

- www.makahiki.kcc.hawaii.edu/tcc/tcc_conf96/gross.html
- www.ksi.cpsc.ucalgary.ca/articles/CSCL95CM/
- www.graphic.org/

RECIPROCAL TEACHING

Originally developed for reading comprehension, reciprocal thinking can be used across the curriculum as a dialogue between the teacher and students or student to student to bring meaning to concepts, textual material, artwork, rules in physical education, discussion points, or other knowledge items. Ultimately, everyone becomes a learner and everyone becomes a teacher.

Examples of Reciprocal Teaching

After studying impressionist art, Ms. Jones sets up students in pairs. They are given several prints of various artists of several genres to determine if the paintings are or are not of impressionist style. The students ask questions of each other like: What brush strokes characterize a given painting? How would a given painting need to be altered to become more impressionist? Why did artists of the paintings use certain techniques?

Why Use Reciprocal Teaching?

- Students become engaged and feel responsible for their own learning and that of peers.
- They go from passive learning to active learning.
- Students learn to generate questions.
- Students gain self-confidence and motivation, improved leadership skills, increased cooperation, and greater initiative.

Where Would a Teacher Use Reciprocal Teaching?

Teachers could use reciprocal teaching in any class, any grade level, where student understanding is shallow and limited to the knowledge level. It helps the teacher differentiate instruction.

How Does a Teacher Use Reciprocal Teaching?

Teachers and students share roles for generating interest, uncovering misunderstanding of material, and increasing breadth and depth of meaning of the discussion point. The teacher asks questions aimed at summarizing, clarifying, or predicting. Students take turns assuming the role of teacher and leading the discussion to develop understanding. Specifically, teachers should:

- Realize that training on how to effectively use questions based on the six levels of Bloom's Taxonomy (knowledge, comprehension, application, analysis, synthesis, and evaluation) is necessary for the students to fully benefit from reciprocal teaching.

- Select the topic for the strategy.
- Provide a brief, focused introduction to the material that students have read.
- Where appropriate, link the new material to previous learnings (this will give added purpose to the learner's reading).
- Model the strategies and support learners in using them.
- Regularly monitor learners' use of higher-ordered thinking.

Brain Compatibility: Do You Agree?

Is there emphasis on context and meaning?	Yes	No
Are the multiple intelligences awakened?	Yes	No
Is there low stress and high enjoyment?	Yes	No
Is there immediate feedback?	Yes	No
Is there active involvement?	Yes	No
Does it provide novelty?	Yes	No

For More Information

- www.utoledo.edu/~kpugh/6-8360/Palincsar.html
- www.sdcoe.k12.ca.us/score/promising/tips/rec.html
- www.mdk12.org/instruction/success_mspap/general/projectbetter/science/s-38-40.html

SIX THINKING HATS

Six Thinking Hats is a strategy developed by Edward DeBono and used in classrooms to help students look at issues from many perspectives. Six different-colored hats refer to different ways of examining a problem or issue, as seen in Figure 3.10.

Examples of Six Thinking Hats

- Science teacher has students look at cloning from the Six Hats perspectives.
- Social studies teacher has students look at the conflict in the Middle East.

- Students in a health class look at the issue of using steroids for athletic performance.
- Art students examine impressionist paintings from the Six Hats perspectives.
- A disciplinary case in which students reflect on behavior from the Six Hats perspectives.

Edward DeBono's Six Hat Thinking

White Hat Thinking

Used to think about facts, figures, and objective information.

Symbol: A scientist's lab coat

Questions: What are the facts? How did I get them?

Hot Thinking

Used to elicit feelings and emotions

Symbol: A heart

Questions: How do I really feel? What is my gut reaction?

Black Hat Thinking

Used to inspire logical, negative arguments - devil's advocate

Symbol: A judge's robe

Questions: What are the possible downside risks and problems?

Yellow Hat Thinking

Used to see the positive outlook - sees opportunities and benefits

Symbol: The warming sun

Questions: What are the advantages?
What is the best possible outcome?

Blue Hat Thinking

Used to state the overreaching idea or gist of the situation

Symbol: The sky

Questions: What have I learned? What is the main idea?

Green Hat Thinking

Used to find creative new ideas

Symbol: New shoots sprouting from seeds

Questions: What are some new innovative solutions?
How can I see the problem in a new way?

Figure 3.10.   Six Thinking Hats

Why Use Six Thinking Hats?

Students typically react to a controversial issue viscerally and emotionally, which is red hat thinking. The Six Hats strategy requires them to use other ways of thinking about problems and issues. It encourages thinking factually, flexibly, logically, creatively, holistically, and heuristically.

Where Would a Teacher Use Six Thinking Hats?

Teachers could use Six Thinking Hats in any class, any grade, and in any situation.

How Does a Teacher Use Six Thinking Hats?

- First, teach students the thinking associated with each of the colors.
- Next, practice with a particular issue using one of the colors. For example, take the issue of computer Internet filtering and apply yellow hat thinking (What are the advantages of filtering?).
- Then, practice with another color on the same issue. For example, use black hat thinking to look at the disadvantages of filtering.
- Continue with each of the colors. This will result in spirited discussion and an amazingly comprehensive range of thinking on an important issue.

Brain Compatibility: Do You Agree?

Is there emphasis on context and meaning?	Yes	No
Are the multiple intelligences awakened?	Yes	No
Is there low stress and high enjoyment?	Yes	No
Is there immediate feedback?	Yes	No
Is there active involvement?	Yes	No
Does it provide novelty?	Yes	No

For More Information

- *Six Thinking Hats* by Edward DeBono
- www.gamos.demon.co.uk/sustainable/hatpap.htm
- www.naturalmaths.com.au/Settings/six_hats.htm

CHOICE BOARDS

Choice board (aka tic-tac-toe or think-tac-toe) is a strategy that enables students to choose tasks to practice a skill or demonstrate and extend understanding of a process or concept. It is an excellent example of the application of Bloom's Taxonomy. From the board (Figure 3.11), students choose (or the teacher assigns) three adjacent or diagonal tasks to complete a tic-tac-toe.

Examples of Choice Boards

Generic Choice Board
(Use Your Own Subject Matter)

Collect	Teach	Draw	Judge
facts or ideas that are important to you. **(Knowledge)**	a lesson about your topic to our class. Include at least one visual aid. **(Synthesis)**	a diagram, map, or picture of your topic. **(Application)**	two different viewpoints about an issue. Explain your decision. **(Evaluation)**
Photograph	Demonstrate	Graph	Create
videotape, or film part of your presentation. **(Synthesis)**	something to show what you have learned. **(Application)**	some part of your study to show how many or how few. **(Analysis)**	an original home, dance, picture, song, or story. Elaborate. **(Synthesis)**
Dramatize	Survey	Forcast	Build
something to show what you have learned. **(Synthesis)**	others to learn their opinions about some fact, idea, or feature of your study. **(Analysis)**	how your topic will change in the next 10 years. **(Synthesis)**	a model or diorama to illustrate what you have learned. **(Application)**
Create	Memorize	Write	Compare
an original game using the facts you have learned.	recite a quote or a short list of facts about your topic.	an editorial for the student newspaper or draw an editorial cartoon. **(Evaluation)**	two things from your study. Look for ways they are alike and different. **(Analysis)**

Figure 3.11. Generic Choice Board

Choice Board—Using Persuasion to Address a Contemporary Issue

Sketch a political cartoon to express your opinion about the issue you have selected. Be sure to use irony to make your point. Give your cartoon a caption.	Write, shoot, and edit a short video showing your position on the issue you have selected. Be sure that both the video and audio portions of your production use persuasive strategies to imply your position clearly and forcefully. (You may select this option instead of any to the left.)	Write and deliver a 3–4-minute persuasive speech arguing your position on the issue you have selected. Be sure to develop an interesting opening and a strong close. Use persuasive strategies to develop your argument, including facts, statistics, and appeals to the audience's emotions and ethics.
Create a poster or posters for a public service announcement related to the issue you have selected. Use your visual design and several persuasive strategies to convince people to agree with your position on the issue.	Using both print and non-print sources, find out as much as you can about this issue. Write a bibliography of all sources you use to research this issue. Turn in all of your notes and highlighted copies of information.	Write an outline of a report stating your position on the issue you have selected and showing the information you have found. Begin your outline with a paragraph stating your position, then use different headings to show your information in outline form. Include a concluding paragraph.
Design several line or bar graphs, pie charts, or tables showing information related to the issue you have selected. You may use a combination of these types of visuals; be sure to label them clearly. Keep in mind that the way information is presented can be a powerful persuasive tool.	Write a two-column script for a political advertisement supporting your position on the issue you have selected. Be sure that both the video and audio portions of your script use persuasive strategies to imply your position clearly and forcefully. (You may select this option instead of any to the right.)	Write a 500–700-word editorial expressing your view on the issue you have chosen. Be sure to use persuasive strategies in your argument, including facts, statistics, and appeals to the reader's emotions and ethics.

Why Use Choice Boards?

The choice board technique is an effective way to differentiate instruction for interests or readiness levels. It honors student options, thereby increasing motivation. Tasks can be tiered for differing abilities. Experience shows that students love this activity for its choices and for the freedom to work individually or in groups.

Where Would a Teacher Use Choice Boards?

Choice boards are easily adapted to any subject area.

How Does a Teacher Use Choice Boards?

- Identify the outcomes and instructional focus using Bloom's *Taxonomy of Educational Objectives, Handbook 1: Cognitive Domain* and student interest.
- Design 9 to 16 different tasks.
- Write the tasks, one task to each square, on a tic-tac-toe board.
- You may want to select one critical task to place in the center of the board for all students to complete, or you may decide to arrange the tasks in rows according to level of difficulty. A better way to arrange the tasks is to follow the model above so that no matter which direction the student completes the straight line, at least one of the tasks will include a higher-level thinking skill of analysis, synthesis, or evaluation.
- Choose activities in a tic-tac-toe design. Students form tic-tac-toe horizontally, vertically, diagonally, or in the four corners. They may decide to be finished or to keep going and complete more activities.
- Students star the activities they plan to complete—in effect, a learning contract—and shade in the box when they finish an activity.
- Teachers can furnish feedback to the student and assess both qualitatively (according to a predetermined rubric) and quantitatively (per standards).

Brain Compatibility: Do You Agree?

Is there emphasis on context and meaning?	Yes	No
Are the multiple intelligences awakened?	Yes	No
Is there low stress and high enjoyment?	Yes	No
Is there immediate feedback?	Yes	No
Is there active involvement?	Yes	No
Does it provide novelty?	Yes	No

For More Information

- *Differentiation in Practice: A Resource Guide for Differentiating Curriculum, Grades 5–9,* by C. A. Tomlinson
- www.wall.k12.nj.us/staff_dev/differentiating_instruction.htm

CUBING

Cubing is a strategy of differentiating or individualizing instruction to help students think at their readiness and interest level about a topic from six perspectives. Cubing refers to a six-sided cube on which questions are written by the teacher or the student on each side of the cube. An example is seen in Figure 3.12. Bloom's Taxonomy furnishes a template for the questions.

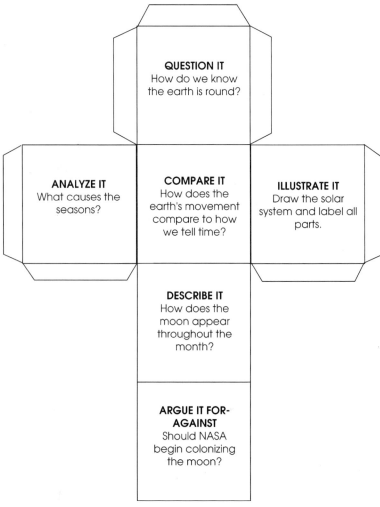

Figure 3.12.   Cubing

Examples of Cubing

- In English class, students choose from among several cubes, each with different levels of difficulty to complete tasks, each of which is written on one side of the cube.
- Science students study the respiratory system through tasks written on each side of the cube.
- Music students study composers of the jazz age by demonstrating the different types of beat and rhythm from each side of the cube.

One example of a cube comes from differentiated instruction and is called a tiered cube. The tiers refer to levels of difficulty. Think of stair steps, where each step takes you to a higher position, as seen in Figure 3.13. Tiered instruction moves students from easier to more challenging levels based on such factors as readiness, past performance, interest, and talent.

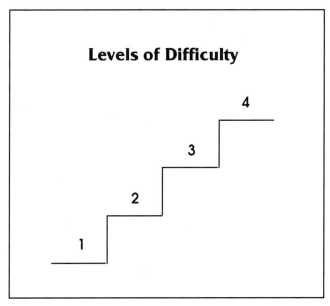

Figure 3.13.   Stairs

Cube 1: Less Challenging	Cube 2: More Challenging	Cube 3: Most Challenging
Side One On the map provided locate the colonial settlement and the Native American settlement. Represent the topography and river systems. If you wish, make a drawing of the two settlements.	Make a chart that contrasts the way in which Native Americans interact with their environment versus the way the Caucasian people interact with their environment by using clear examples from the book.	Write a paragraph or a poem that contrasts how the two cultures' attitudes toward nature affect the way they interact with nature.
Side Two Develop a timeline that includes at least 10 important events from the novel. Write a brief explanation for each justifying why you think it is so significant.	Decide what you consider to be the three most important events that lead to the climax of the book. Identify them and explain how they build suspense.	Describe the climax of the novel and explain why the author selected that climax.
Side Three Explain the Native American view of education and then describe the colonists' requirements for education. Point out similarities and/or differences.	Make a chart that compares the ways in which the Native Americans raise their children to the colonists' approach to raising their children.	Decide which approach to educating children was the most effective: that of the Native Americans, or that of the colonists. Write a persuasive paragraph defending your position.
Side Four Make two scrolls that contain: 1. The codes and rules by which the Native Americans lived, made decisions, and governed themselves. 2. The codes and rules by which the colonists lived and made decisions.	Describe two major decisions made by the colonists and two made by the Native Americans. Compare the process each group used for making those decisions, including the roles played by the leaders in each group and the advantages/disadvantages of each.	Write two fully developed paragraphs explaining your answer to the following two questions: 1. Why did the decision to banish True Son have to be made? 2. Did the Native Americans have a true democracy?
Side Five Make a chart that compares the advantages that True Son found about Native American life with the disadvantages that he found with colonial life.	If you had written this novel, how would you have ended it? Provide at least two well supported reasons to justify your decision.	You have decided to write a sequel to this novel that describes True Son's life after he was banished. Describe the key aspects of your sequel, providing a justification for each.
Side Six Make a visual or a log that shows/describes the most important symbols of the Native American culture and those of the colonial culture. Be prepared to explain why you made your selections.	Make a graphic representation that shows what the Native American culture valued most and one that shows what the colonists valued most.	Decide whether or not the book's title is appropriate. If necessary change the title and write at least one paragraph justifying your decision.

Figure 3.14. Cubing Levels

Figure 3.14, using the example of *The Light in the Forest* by Conrad Richter, represents three different cubes. Read vertically to see one set level of difficulty; read horizontally to see how the activities address the same objective but increase in difficulty, which yields three cubes at different levels. (Note: For additional activities using this novel, see *The Light in the Forest: A Unit Plan* by Barbara M. Linde.)

Why Use Cubing?

Cubing is another way to support both multiple intelligences and Bloom's Taxonomy. It provides novelty and student choice, both appreciated by the brain! It frees the teacher to work with small groups of students.

Where Would a Teacher Use Cubing?

Teachers could use cubing in any class as an energizing activity.

How Does a Teacher Use Cubing?

- Make a cardboard cube. A cube-shaped tissue box, covered with plain paper, works well.
- Write on each side such key words as: Draw a mind map, Argue for, Debate, Question, Sequence, Explain, Prepare, Analyze, Design, Build, Write.
- Determine a topic from your subject that lends itself to multiple activities.
- Student can work on cubes individually or in groups.
- Toss the cube to a student. Wherever the student's right thumb grasps the cube is the assigned task.
- Then the cube is tossed to another individual or group.

Brain Compatibility: Do You Agree?

Is there emphasis on context and meaning?	Yes	No
Are the multiple intelligences awakened?	Yes	No
Is there low stress and high enjoyment?	Yes	No
Is there immediate feedback?	Yes	No
Is there active involvement?	Yes	No
Does it provide novelty?	Yes	No

For More Information

- www.bsu.edu/teachers/services/ctr/javits/Instruction/Cubing.htm
- *Differentiation in Practice: A Resource Guide for Differentiating Curriculum, Grades 5–9* by C. A. Tomlinson
- www.mcps.k12.md.us/departments/eii/diffexemplaryex.html#Cubing

STRUCTURED NOTE TAKING

Structured note taking is using a template to help students process what they hear and make sense of their notes. It uses a form provided by the teacher or by simply drawing a vertical line down the center of the page and placing key words and main ideas on the left. On the right side, students write details amplifying the concepts on the left side. At the bottom of the page, students write a summary (see Figure 3.15).

Example of Structured Note Taking

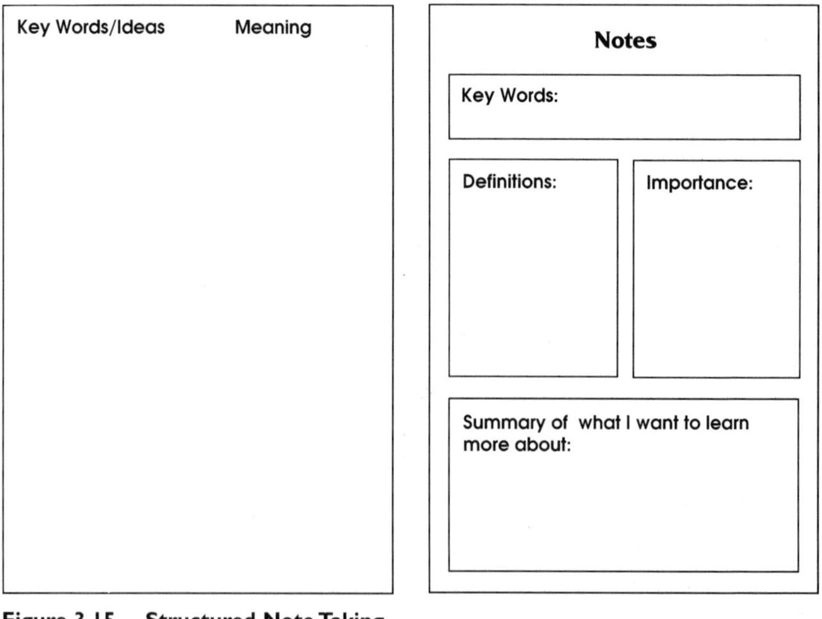

Figure 3.15.   Structured Note Taking

Why Use Structured Note Taking?

As students take notes during a presentation or reading, they have a way to organize their writing. This helps students structure their thinking and leads to greater understanding and reflection on the topic. It makes it easier to review notes and prepare for tests.

Where Would a Teacher Use Structured Note Taking?

Teachers would use structured note taking in any class where the teacher expects students to take notes as a way to emphasize learning or to reinforce material to be mastered.

How Does a Teacher Use Structured Note Taking?

- Observe student note taking and analyze weaknesses.
- Create a template for note taking that organizes key content.
- Have students practice using the template with easy material.
- Provide templates for students to use thereafter with normal lessons.
- Examine results and show students good examples.

Brain Compatibility: Do You Agree?

Is there emphasis on context and meaning?	Yes	No
Are the multiple intelligences awakened?	Yes	No
Is there low stress and high enjoyment?	Yes	No
Is there immediate feedback?	Yes	No
Is there active involvement?	Yes	No
Does it provide novelty?	Yes	No

For More Information

- www.web.odu.edu/webroot/orgs/Educ/Misc/MCTP.nsf/pages/ eci795mctp_nalp (Note: This site offers an acclaimed strategy for teachers to use in developing an effective presentation, called the New American Lecture. It offers a comprehensive template for teacher planning but could be adapted for students.)
- www.somers.k12.ny.us/intranet/reading/structuredideas.html
- http://homepage.tinet.ie/~denisdunne1/homework/k05.htm

DEBATE

Debate is a discussion of an issue in which pros and cons are presented either formally or informally. It can fit in a single class period or longer for a more thorough exposition of different viewpoints.

Examples of Debate

- Teams choose sides on an ethical issue: How far should scientists be permitted to experiment in the field of cloning?
- Students choose positions for or against teenage curfews.
- Class teams debate "Should the U.S. send manned flights to Mars?"

Why Use Debate?

Debates help students develop their critical thinking and research skills, engage in the course materials, and get practice in speaking and listening. Students gain a deeper understanding of a topic while learning other perspectives. Debates are a natural with students. They generally love to argue and to participate in pro and con discussions. It can make for a lively classroom.

Where Would a Teacher Use Debate?

Teachers could use debate in any class where they wish to expand student conceptual thinking. Ethical issues can be addressed with debates, such as the pros and cons of the military draft.

How Does a Teacher Use Debate?

- Select an issue of interest to students. This may emerge from topic of study, an item in the news, a spontaneous argument in the class, or an issue of school policy.
- Have students research the issue by learning how others have addressed the topic, searching the Internet, reading for information, conducting surveys, and making pro and con charts, as in the example shown in Figure 3.16.

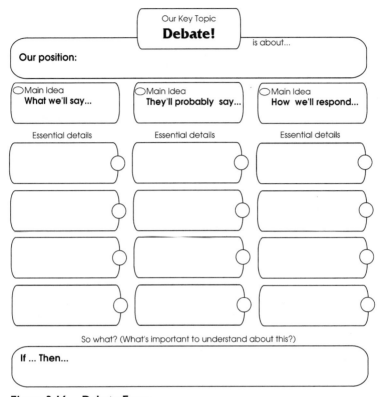

Our Key Topic
Debate!
is about...

Our position:

○Main Idea
What we'll say...

○Main Idea
They'll probably say...

○Main Idea
How we'll respond...

Essential details

Essential details

Essential details

So what? (What's important to understand about this?)

If ... Then...

Figure 3.16. Debate Form

- Help students state the issue conceptually into a positive statement.
- Establish ground rules for the degree of debate formality and procedures. Conduct the debates, if formal, according to Figure 3.17.
- Discuss:
  - the strongest points
  - how well the topic was researched
  - how well arguments were presented
  - the degree of decorum and respect paid opponents
- Consider a rubric on such points as:
  - eye contact
  - voice quality
  - organization of points

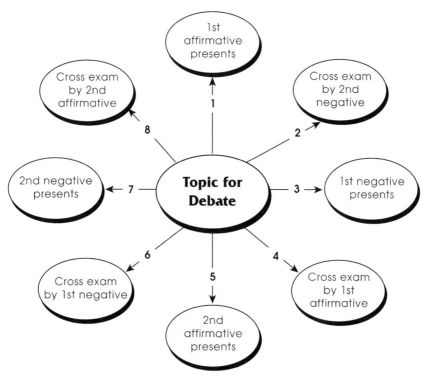

Figure 3.17.   Debate Procedure

- merits of arguments
- adequacy of research
- emotional appeal
- confidence of speakers
- overall effectiveness
- Reflect with students on the merits of studying a topic with the debate strategy.

Brain Compatibility: Do You Agree?

Is there emphasis on context and meaning?	Yes	No
Are the multiple intelligences awakened?	Yes	No
Is there low stress and high enjoyment?	Yes	No
Is there immediate feedback?	Yes	No
Is there active involvement?	Yes	No
Does it provide novelty?	Yes	No

For More Information

- www.chemheritage.org/EducationalServices/pharm/tg/chemo/activity/debate.htm
- www.perfectionlearning.com/mcd/mcd.tm.pdf
- www.fieldsofhope.org/teachers/activity_7.asp

NOMINAL GROUP PROCESS

The nominal group process is a strategy for helping students set goals, define and solve problems, and brainstorm issues. The teacher monitors the discussion, keeps the group working, ensures that everyone participates, and helps the group reach consensus.

Examples of Nominal Group Process

- Health class discussion of the various dieting methods
- Students share solutions on funding of presidential elections
- Students brainstorm ways to get involved in the community

Why Use Nominal Group Process?

Nominal group process increases interaction among students, encourages problem solving, enhances critical thinking, and compares responses with different points of view.

Where Would a Teacher Use Nominal Group Process?

Nominal group process can be used in any class for discussion of a key question or issue to increase interest and motivation.

How Does a Teacher Use Nominal Group Process?

- Have students write individual responses to the question or problem posed.
- Divide students into teams of four to five members.

- Each group has a leader and recorder.
- In round-robin fashion, team members share their ideas without comment other than clarification.
- Teams rank-order their ideas.
- Teams share their ideas with other teams.
- Post all ideas on the board.
- Students debate their responses to continue the interaction and learning.

Brain Compatibility: Do You Agree?

Is there emphasis on context and meaning?	Yes	No
Are the multiple intelligences awakened?	Yes	No
Is there low stress and high enjoyment?	Yes	No
Is there immediate feedback?	Yes	No
Is there active involvement?	Yes	No
Does it provide novelty?	Yes	No

For More Information

- www.extension.iastate.edu/communities/tools/decisions/nominal.html
- www.msue.msu.edu/msue/imp/modii/iii00005.html
- www.oznet.ksu.edu/LEADS/FACT%20Sheets/fact2.pdf

THINK-PAIR-SHARE

Think-Pair-Share (a simpler version of nominal group process) is a strategy to get students to think about an issue using intrapersonal and interpersonal intelligences. Think-Pair-Share is one of the most common cooperative learning strategies, and one of the easiest to use.

Examples of Think-Pair-Share

- In science class: How can our school be more environmentally conscious?
- In math: List the geometric applications used in building the school.

- In English language learning: What challenges are faced by minority cultures in the United States?

Why Use Think-Pair-Share?

The structure is extremely versatile because it can be used for higher-level thinking, as well as basic review and recall.

- All students are involved. It can engage several of the multiple intelligences.
- Any student will feel rewarded by seeing his or her idea emerge in the final version.
- This strategy can be used on the spur of the moment and is non-threatening.
- Discussion of an idea with a partner helps clarify or correct ideas and thinking.

Where Would a Teacher Use Think-Pair-Share?

Think-Pair-Share can be used in any class for discussing an idea.

How Does a Teacher Use Think-Pair-Share?

- Teacher states the issue or problem.
- Each student writes down an idea or two.
- Students tell their ideas to their partner.
- Student listens attentively to partner's idea.
- Partners switch roles.
- Class discussion of the ideas from partners.

Brain Compatibility: Do You Agree?

Is there emphasis on context and meaning?	Yes	No
Are the multiple intelligences awakened?	Yes	No
Is there low stress and high enjoyment?	Yes	No
Is there immediate feedback?	Yes	No
Is there active involvement?	Yes	No
Does it provide novelty?	Yes	No

For More Information

- www.home.att.net/~clnetwork/thinkps.htm
- www.curry.edschool.virginia.edu/go/edis771/notes/THNKPRSH
.html
- *Differentiated Instructional Strategies: One Size Doesn't Fit All* by
Gayle Gregory and Carolyn Chapman

MENTAL IMAGING

Mental imaging is creating a picture in the student's mind of the steps
to complete a task at hand. Students mentally run through the task, performing it perfectly in their mind and feeling great satisfaction.

Examples of Mental Imaging

- Science students mentally practice the steps of dissecting a frog.
- Spanish students mentally practice visiting and ordering a meal at
a restaurant.
- Basketball players mentally practice free throws.
- Practical arts students mentally practice the actions of using tools.
- Art students create their product in their mind before the actual
activity.

Why Use Mental Imaging?

Psychologically, learners will tend to be more successful if they can
form a mental image of what they need to do. Successful coaches at all
levels use this technique to improve athletic performance.

Where Would a Teacher Use Mental Imaging?

This strategy has application for any subject area. Though seldom
used, it has great power to improve performance.

How Does a Teacher Use Mental Imaging?

- Student identifies each step and labels each step of the task being
practiced.

- A mental picture is formed of the self performing each step successfully.
- Student mentally judges each step of the task according to criteria furnished by the teacher.
- At completion of task, the student conducts an overall evaluation based on criteria.
- Student must pay particular attention to feelings of satisfaction from perfect mental performance.
- Upon successful mental performance, students practice real time, real world.

Brain Compatibility: Do You Agree?

Is there emphasis on context and meaning?	Yes	No
Are the multiple intelligences awakened?	Yes	No
Is there low stress and high enjoyment?	Yes	No
Is there immediate feedback?	Yes	No
Is there active involvement?	Yes	No
Does it provide novelty?	Yes	No

For More Information

- www.eteamz.com/baseball/instruction/pitching/clinic.cfm/Mental%20Imaging/
- www.t4.jordan.k12.ut.us/Balanced_Literacy/Comprehension/cs_mental_imaging.htm
- *Imaging for Students* by David Lisle

KWHL STRATEGY

The KWHL strategy aims to help students use knowledge they have acquired. It is a variation of the well-known strategy known as KWL.

- K stands for What do we already *know*?
- W for *What* do we want to learn?
- H for *How* can find the information?
- L for What have we *learned*?

Examples of KWHL

- Student knowledge and interest in the Civil War
- Preparation for a new unit on sonnets
- Seeing what student know about simple equations in math

Why Use KWHL?

- KWHL, a group instruction technique, serves to activate prior knowledge.
- Brain compatibility comes in by tapping the collective knowledge students have of a concept or topic, thus showing students the connections they already have.
- It also exposes misconceptions so that the teacher can more accurately plan and design instruction based on gaps in knowledge.

Where Would a Teacher Use KWHL?

KWHL can be used in any class, either prior to instruction on a new topic to learn what students presently know or after a unit to assess understanding.

How Does a Teacher Use KWHL?

- Teacher must have clear learning outcomes that are shared with students.
- Teacher records on a chart or board student responses to the first two questions: What do you already know? and What do you want to learn? Teacher will often need to ask probing questions as a way to prod students' responses. An alternative is to have student groups record their responses on a handout chart (see Figure 3.18).
- Teacher and students brainstorm about how they will find information.
- The teacher uses this information to design learning experiences.
- At the completion of the unit, students respond to the last question: What have you learned?

- If interest remains, the teacher determines next steps, resources, and other activities.
- For example, use Figure 3.18 to set up a study of the solar system.

Brain Compatibility: Do You Agree?

Is there emphasis on context and meaning?	Yes	No
Are the multiple intelligences awakened?	Yes	No
Is there low stress and high enjoyment?	Yes	No
Is there immediate feedback?	Yes	No
Is there active involvement?	Yes	No
Does it provide novelty?	Yes	No

For More Information

- www.ncrel.org/sdrs/areas/issues/students/learning/lr1kwlh.htm
- www.ncwiseowl.org/webquest/spider/Spider%20WebQuest%20KWLH%20Handout.html
- www.pwcs.edu/curriculum/sol/kwl.htm

SOCRATIC SEMINAR

Socratic seminar is a dialogue based on a piece of text that addresses a critical question. It is open-ended; the only rule is that students must be courteous of each other. It involves opposing views, debating, and persuading. The topic should be one that has no right or wrong answer.

What Do We Already Know?	What Do We Want to Learn?	How Can We Find Information?	What Have We Learned?

Figure 3.18.   KWHL Chart

Examples of Socratic Seminar (Generic Questions)

- Does the text agree or disagree with this statement?
- What does the term ___ mean?
- In what ways are ___ and ___ alike and different?
- What might be some other good titles?
- This passage seems to contradict __. Agree or disagree?
- How does this passage connect to ___ (refer to another passage or text)?
- What are the inferences?
- What are the implications?
- How did you arrive at your view?

Why Use Socratic Seminar?

Students learn to examine ideas rationally, to explore, and to process new ideas. It assumes that many people have pieces of answers and can lead to peaceable solutions. Dialogue creates conditions of open-mindedness and an interchange of views and questioning.

Where Would a Teacher Use Socratic Seminar?

Socratic seminars precede discussions in any class dealing with thought-provoking questions.

How Does a Teacher Use Socratic Seminar?

- Assign a piece of text (1–12 pages) to read and study. Students are encouraged to underline passages, write questions in the margin, and summarize the meaning.
- Arrange students in a circle for good interaction.
- Give students x number (say, three) of buttons (any token) as a device to ensure that all students have opportunities to participate. Students surrender a button each time they speak.
- Ask a series of questions that give direction to the dialogue. Rephrase questions until they are understood.
- Ensure the flow of dialogue with the teacher as a participant.
- Ask questions that allow for a range of answers.

- Allow for conflict or differences of views.
- Examine answers and draw out implications.
- Request reasons for answers.
- Remain open to questions raised by answers.
- Present all sides of an argument.
- Do not insist on common agreement.

Brain Compatibility: Do You Agree?

Is there emphasis on context and meaning?	Yes	No
Are the multiple intelligences awakened?	Yes	No
Is there low stress and high enjoyment?	Yes	No
Is there immediate feedback?	Yes	No
Is there active involvement?	Yes	No
Does it provide novelty?	Yes	No

For More Information

- www.ncrel.org/sdrs/areas/issues/students/learning/lr2refer.htm
- www.socraticseminars.com/whatare.htm
- www.studyguide.org/socratic_seminar.htm (This site has an excellent rubric for judging student participation.)

GALLERY WALK

In gallery walk, students add comments, answers, or solutions to posed questions or topics written on newsprint mounted on the wall by circulating clockwise around the room. A variation is called Table Talk where students go from table to table.

Examples of Gallery Walk

- Students evaluate peer work after the completion of a project by visiting each project and making written comments and suggestions.
- In social studies, after studying the Great Depression, students circulate individually or in groups to respond to such questions as:
  - What was the political climate?
  - What were the living conditions of average citizens?

- What was the impact on the arts?
- What happened in other countries?
- Under what conditions could a depression happen today?

Why Use Gallery Walk?

Gallery walk generates many solutions and answers to questions. It energizes a class and provides for creativity. It lets the teacher see immediately how much students have learned or mislearned.

Where Would a Teacher Use Gallery Walk?

Any teacher can use this strategy to introduce a topic or to summarize what was learned.

How Does a Teacher Use Gallery Walk?

- Questions are posed on newsprint (one per sheet) and posted around the room.
- Students in groups write answers or solutions to the question on the newsprint.
- Students rotate clockwise to the next sheet at a given signal.
- When students return to their initial sheet, they organize the information.
- Students report their summary to the entire group.
- Teachers can build on the reports to summarize or clarify misunderstandings.
- A variation: Students write a question on a 5×7 card and it circulates around the table with each person adding an answer or solution.

Brain Compatibility: Do You Agree?		
Is there emphasis on context and meaning?	Yes	No
Are the multiple intelligences awakened?	Yes	No
Is there low stress and high enjoyment?	Yes	No
Is there immediate feedback?	Yes	No
Is there active involvement?	Yes	No
Does it provide novelty?	Yes	No

For More Information

- www.edservices.aea7.k12.ia.us/framework/strategies/
- www.concordhs.com/ateachsite/processing/gallerywalk.pdf
- www.post1.com/home/garytsu/ITLessonProcess.htm

SQ3R

SQ3R is an enduring strategy for reading in content areas. To help military personnel undergoing accelerated university courses, Francis Robinson, a psychologist, invented SQ3R during World War II. It worked well. It still works well, especially for texts you must understand thoroughly and remember completely. With the emphasis on all teachers providing reading instruction in their content area, this strategy is particularly useful. S stands for *Survey*, Q stands for *Question*, and 3R refers to R for *Read*, R for *Recite*, R for *Review*.

Examples of SQ3R

- Science assigned reading passage on DNA
- Physical education text on rules of badminton
- Music background chapter on culture of an era

Why Use SQ3R?

Students use SQ3R to increase reading efficiency and comprehension. SQ3R gives students specific steps that make text understandable.

Where Would a Teacher Use SQ3R?

Teachers would use SQ3R in any content that involves student interpreting and retaining understanding from reading.

How Does a Teacher Use SQ3R?

- *Survey*: Students preview the reading assignment by noting headings, introduction, illustrations, and the summary. This gives students a general idea of the material.

- *Question*: Turn the heading or subtitle into a question before reading each section. This gives the students a purpose for reading the material.
- *Read*: The students then read each section to learn answers to their questions.
- *Recite*: After reading each section, students should again review their question from the heading or subtitle and verify their answer by reciting it in their own words. Students may check their notes or underlinings.
- *Review*: After finishing the entire assignment, review each of the headings or subtitles and try to remember the answers to their questions.

Brain Compatibility: Do You Agree?

Is there emphasis on context and meaning?	Yes	No
Are the multiple intelligences awakened?	Yes	No
Is there low stress and high enjoyment?	Yes	No
Is there immediate feedback?	Yes	No
Is there active involvement?	Yes	No
Does it provide novelty?	Yes	No

For More Information

- www.u.arizona.edu/ic/wrightr/other/sq3r.html
- www.accd.edu/sac/history/keller/ACCDitg/SSSQ3R.htm
- www.accessexcellence.org/AE/newatg/Haugen.sq3rplus/

4

LEARNING STRATEGIES

Learning strategies assume that engaged students will learn more. Obviously, teaching strategies aim for the same result. The difference, though admittedly tenuous, stems from the locus of control, and also from the authors' desire to more clearly delineate between what are essentially teacher-controlled learning activities versus more student-directed activities. The distinction, though important, may not look that different in terms of classroom practice. Both are student centered. There is greater overlap than there are clear differences, as this chapter's learning activities must be selected and ultimately controlled by the teacher.

We offer these learning strategies as a potent addition to the previous chapter's teaching strategies. Be patient with these strategies. Experience with their use will sharpen your knowledge of what to attend to for greater effectiveness. Any strategy takes time to hone its details. These strategies powerfully focus student learning and energy. They incite motivation and learning.

Several essential questions arise for schools that use practices following the general principles of this chapter. These questions are particularly pertinent given the national movements on standards, testing, and accountability. Critical questions include:

- Will students learn more?
- What will students learn more of?
- What will students learn less of?
- Is that a good trade-off?
- Will students enjoy school more?
- Will students be more engaged?
- Will students be prepared for their roles as citizens, workers, and lifelong learners?
- Will there be fewer destructive and self-defeating behaviors by students?

The answers to these and similar questions can be found in research studies and the practices of a wide variety of schools over many decades. Clearly, it serves no one well if schools can't obtain useful answers to essential questions. Although beyond the scope of this book, the reader might review such material as the famous Eight-Year Study (Aiken, 1942), the work of such groups as the National Association for Core Curriculum or the Association for Experiential Education, and the results of experimental schools. We believe the practices described in this book are congruent with valid research studies and help ensure vital school outcomes.

COMMITTEES AND TASK FORCES

Students are divided into small groups of about four to six members to work on a complex project or task, primarily at their own pace and direction. A variation of this strategy is the well-known approach of cooperative learning.

Examples of Committees and Task Forces

- A four-student group works for several weeks trying to figure out the causes of welfare. They make a presentation on their findings.

- A small group of students prepares recommendations about problems of drugs in athletics.
- Five students write a skit on the reactions of sodium with other chemicals.

Why Use Committees and Task Forces?

Students enjoy working together and gain valuable skills in doing so. For example, students develop leadership skills by sensing directly what works and what doesn't in assigning and carrying out the subtasks of the larger goal. They learn the important lesson that each person has different skills and talents, such as interviewing, writing, illustrating, or speaking. This is great training for how the world conducts itself, such as when work teams and community groups gather information, determine findings, and make recommendations. The engagement of learners in a good working committee is higher than during lectures or class discussions because minds are active and a level of excitement prevails as people dig for information, solve problems, organize ideas, make discoveries, and teach others what they have learned.

Where Would a Teacher Use Committees and Task Forces?

Committees and task forces can be used for any topic of some complexity—that is, any topic without a simple answer.

How Does a Teacher Use Committees and Task Forces?

Teachers who have tried committees often report that students waste a lot of time, are off-task, or shoot the breeze, or that just one or two members do all the work. Without training, that can happen. It also happens if students are not really interested in the topic or it seems like make-work to them.

Here is a suggestion for the problem of unproductive committees. Have students brainstorm (in small groups) a list of what a dysfunctional committee would be like. What would an ineffective committee spend its time doing? How would members act? What would they accomplish? Then have each of the small groups give their ideas and jot them down on the board. Have one or two volunteers make a poster of the ideas to post on the wall. Repeat the exercise for what a high-performing group would be like. Post the second chart alongside the first. Take time to talk about how the groups did these two simple tasks. Did they discover any talents or how could they have used special abilities? For example, did they observe skills in leadership, taking turns, skirting dominating members, writing, or drawing? These skills need to be built and reviewed from time to time. The processing time will be well spent.

A second suggestion is to avoid having committees do homework-type tasks. Students should own the topic. It needs to be of interest. The topic might be one that they had a hand in determining or choosing from a list of topics. Teachers can generate such a list with student input by asking what students know about the unit or want to learn about the topic using the KWHL strategy discussed in chapter 3.

Brain Compatibility: Do You Agree?

Is there emphasis on context and meaning?	Yes	No
Are the multiple intelligences awakened?	Yes	No
Is there low stress and high enjoyment?	Yes	No
Is there immediate feedback?	Yes	No
Is there active involvement?	Yes	No
Does it provide novelty?	Yes	No

For More Information

- *Cooperative Learning* by Spencer Kagan and Celso Rodriguez
- *Community Learning Centers* by W. Jennings.
- www.coe.sdsu.edu/eet/Articles/jigsaw/index.htm

PERSONAL LEARNING PLANS

Personal learning plans contain directions to shape a student's school life. They are similar to the individual education plans (IEP) used in special education but far less formalistic. They are a brief document (usually one page or so) listing a student's interest areas, areas of strength, and areas for growth. Based on these items, they include several goals and ways of accomplishing the goals with a suggested timeline. What makes a personal learning plan work is that it is collaboratively written *with* the student, not *about* the student or *for* the student. See Figure 4.1 for an example of a simple personal learning plan.

Why Use Personal Learning Plans?

Personal learning plans make the teacher and the school more aware of student interests and needs. More importantly, the teacher learns of the student's goals and plans. Instructional activities are more

---

Personal Learning Plan
Student-Parent-Advisor Agreement

Student _____ Advisor _____ Date _____

Parent _____   **Review Dates**

1. List learning experiences outside of school such as: home responsibilities, jobs, hobbies, interests, extra-curricular activities, travel experiences, volunteer experiences, reading, and classes.

2. List learning factors:

    I like to do:

    My strengths are:

    I need to learn about:

    My learning styles and intelligneces are:

    My future plans are:

3. Learning goals for this year:

4. What needs to happen to accomplish these goals:

    At. school:

    Outside school:

4. Other comments:

I understand the program and agree to do my best to make a success of my educational opportunities:

Student signature _____ Date _____

Figure 4.1.   Personal Learning Plan

easily tailored and more successful if they take student interest and well-being into account.

Where Would a Teacher Use Personal Learning Plans?

Personal learning plans have been used in almost any grade level, but they work best in elementary schools with a self-contained classroom system and in secondary schools with strong advisor–advisee programs.

How Does a Teacher Use Personal Learning Plans?

It is best if an entire school adopts a program of personal learning plans. That means establishing times for parent-student-teacher/advisor conferences. Ideally, conferences would be held at the start at the beginning of year—actually, just before the first day of school. Such conferences, successfully run, will have a thoughtful discussion while completing the personal learning plan form. Subsequent conferences during the year and at the end of the year are used to review the personal learning form for progress and to determine if modifications are necessary. We have found that progress conferences are best led by the student. That means the students are reporting on their progress and are accountable for their learning plan. Students can be helped in this process with a brief rehearsal and in time will become quite adept at describing their progress, clarifying their goals, and establishing more specific and appropriate goals.

Brain Compatibility: Do You Agree?

Is there emphasis on context and meaning?	Yes	No
Are the multiple intelligences awakened?	Yes	No
Is there low stress and high enjoyment?	Yes	No
Is there immediate feedback?	Yes	No
Is there active involvement?	Yes	No
Does it provide novelty?	Yes	No

For More Information

- www.bigpicture.org/MetPort96-7personalizedLearning.htm
- *Community Learning Centers* by W. Jennings.
- *Inciting Learning* by Joan Caulfield and Wayne Jennings

LEADERSHIP CAMPS

A leadership camp generally occurs in an off-school setting or, if in school, a nonclassroom setting such as the gym. Camp implies an informal environment with an extended setting—for example, sitting on the ground or the floor or in a circle—with activities over several days. Leadership camps need skilled adults for conducting activities with gusto and excitement.

Examples of Leadership Camps

- Student councils use leadership camps to generate spirit, teamwork, and motivation to help make their school the best it can be.
- An interdisciplinary team of four teachers and their 100 students go to a retreat to work out details of how the group can have an extraordinary year.
- At a retreat setting, students and staff are trained to establish a peer counseling program for their school.

Why Use Leadership Camps?

Use leadership camps to build spirit, to generate energy, and to break the mold of student passivity. Students have great reserves of learning power and drive that can be awakened and revitalized. The nontraditional setting, energizing activities, and high degree of active participation lift students from lethargy to new levels of vigor and interest.

Where Would a Teacher Use a Leadership Camp?

An individual class might go into "camp" mode in order to settle serious structure problems of disinterest or dysfunction. The normal operating mode would be suspended to address critical issues for success. Any class or program might profit from such an activity.

How Does a Teacher Use a Leadership Camp?

The leadership camp strategy requires much planning. It's probably best planned with a team from the staff, working with a skilled facilitator.

Experienced student council advisors are familiar with camps. School administration needs to provide support and to clear obstacles, especially if other classes are in session at the same time.

Brain Compatibility: Do You Agree?		
Is there emphasis on context and meaning?	Yes	No
Are the multiple intelligences awakened?	Yes	No
Is there low stress and high enjoyment?	Yes	No
Is there immediate feedback?	Yes	No
Is there active involvement?	Yes	No
Does it provide novelty?	Yes	No

For More Information

- www.principals.org/pdf/nlc_2004brochure.pdf
- www.nhs.us/pdf/nslc04_adultstaffapp.doc
- www.media3.iss.indiana.edu/htbin/wwform/www/?TEXT=R1827 9575-18283259-/www/documents/188/cat/wwi770.htm

ROLE-PLAYING

Role-playing is simulating a person or situation so that it can be examined, analyzed, and better understood.

Examples of Role-Playing:

- Students make a skit of how it feels to be ignored.
- A student takes the role of Douglas MacArthur on hearing he has been relieved of his command by the president of the United States.
- Students practice their part in the upcoming parent–student–advisor conferences in which each will lead the session.

Why Use Role-Playing?

Role-playing is one of the most engaging activities, as the entire group will watch and analyze the role-play with great interest. They mentally play the same role and think how they might have handled the situation. They quickly identify with an issue because the role-play almost automatically draws them in, whether as one of the players or onlookers. Students get "outside" themselves to look at a situation with lessened fear or embarrassment since they aren't being themselves but just playing a role. Students enjoy watching other students.

Where Would a Teacher Use Role-Playing?

Any class can use skits or dramatic incidents to reinforce or deepen learning.

How Does a Teacher Use Role-Playing?

A teacher may ask, for example, how you think the character in a novel (or with a current event) might have handled the situation differently. Rather than just discussion, ask who would like to take the part of the characters and play it out differently. You could combine role-playing with committees and have each group come up with a skit or interpretation.

Brain Compatibility: Do You Agree?

Is there emphasis on context and meaning?	Yes	No
Are the multiple intelligences awakened?	Yes	No
Is there low stress and high enjoyment?	Yes	No
Is there immediate feedback?	Yes	No
Is there active involvement?	Yes	No
Does it provide novelty?	Yes	No

For More Information

- *Acting, Learning, and Change: Creating Original Plays with Adolescents* by Jan Mandell with Jennifer Lynn Wolf
- *Theater Games for the Classroom: A Teacher's Handbook* by Viola Spolin
- http://216.239.37.104/search?q=cache:JKHH741Mzg0J:www.standards.dfes.gov.uk/literacy/publications/framework/818497/pns062_2003s_lposters.PDF+classroom+drama&hl=en&ie=UTF-8

COMMUNITY SERVICE

Community service, often referred to as service learning, is the placing of students in community agencies, businesses, schools, or other situations beyond the school's operation so that students learn by direct participation about how aspects of the world function.

Examples of Community Service

- Students tutor younger students at a nearby elementary school.
- Students serve a few hours a week at locales such as a hospital, shelter, or fish hatchery.
- Students shovel snow or mow lawns for the elderly near the school.

Why Use Community Service?

Placement where students assume responsibility in real-world settings teaches responsibility, how adults function, and how important tasks are fulfilled. They begin to understand how their skills, interests, and inclinations will serve them in the future. They see directly that work is largely without the glamorization and unrealistic degree of excitement that television portrays. Career aspirations may be formed and perhaps some lines of work will be found uninteresting—an important outcome.

Where Would a Teacher Use Community Service?

Teachers can use community service in any class. For example, a math teacher might have students spend some time in architects' or engineers' offices or carpenter job sites to see the application of math to life. Use community service to bring reality and life to school subjects.

How Does a Teacher Use Community Service?

Community service requires schedule flexibility. It would be impossible to go from third period to a site a mile from school, have significant participation at the site, and make it back to school for a fourth-period class. Some traditionally scheduled schools arrange for community service at the beginning or end of the day by using some school time and some student personal time. Other schools establish schedules that permit leaving classes once a week, say—Wednesday afternoons. Some schools employ a person to assist teachers in community placements. It is best to place students in situations where the interest of the student is greatest. Some states mandate a certain number of hours of community service for graduation in the same manner traditional subjects are required. Give school credit for community service to recognize the essential value of the program. Students involved in community service need opportunities to debrief and reflect on their experiences in order to obtain maximum benefit from their service. They can remark on critical questions such as: What made the experience good (or poor)? Could they have made it better? How effectively did they interact with adults in situations? What makes a good worker at their service site? What key lessons were learned from the community service experience?

Brain Compatibility: Do You Agree?

Is there emphasis on context and meaning?	Yes	No
Are the multiple intelligences awakened?	Yes	No
Is there low stress and high enjoyment?	Yes	No
Is there immediate feedback?	Yes	No
Is there active involvement?	Yes	No
Does it provide novelty?	Yes	No

For More Information

- www.servicelearning.org/
- www.learningindeed.org/index.html
- *The Complete Guide to Service Learning: Proven, Practical Ways to Engage Students in Civic Responsibility, Academic Curriculum, and Social Action* by Cathryn Berger Kaye

EXCHANGES

Exchanges are spending time in another setting, such as between two schools or in another community or country.

Examples of Exchanges

- Students from urban schools spend two weeks in a rural school and vice versa.
- Students have yearlong exchanges between countries for individual students.
- Students spend a day in a school across town with different demographics.

Why Use Exchanges?

Exchanges expose students to new settings and interrupt stereotypic thinking. Students come to see and understand people they previously didn't know and for whom they may have had incorrect notions. They see similarities among people's issues. They begin to understand another cultural setting. Exchanges can be among the most important experiences a student will have in school.

Where Would a Teacher Use Exchanges?

Teachers use exchanges to deepen understanding of other cultures by taking students from the known and comfortable environs of their own culture and immersing them into another cultural situation, thus requiring the student to adapt to new conditions.

How Does a Teacher Use Exchanges?

Although exchanges pay off in student understandings of other points of view, they require a great deal of preparation, ranging from simple one-day exchanges with another school to those involving, say, two weeks in another city. First, the teacher must be clear about the purposes of the exchange and be able to communicate the purposes to students and their parents. Exchanges involving several days to weeks should be done one school at a time; that is, one school does the exchange and, later, the other school does the return exchange. Such exchanges require written permission from parents. Paperwork includes such information as medical conditions, medical contacts, permission to take medical action in an emergency if parents are not reachable, and a notice that students will be sent home at their parents' expense if serious disciplinary problems arise. When students stay with other families, the receiving school approves the family's participation. Food and costs are borne by the receiving family, except for transportation to the site. Students attend the other school just as they would their own school. School administration and school board approval are essential to success and meeting legal requirements.

Brain Compatibility: Do You Agree?

Is there emphasis on context and meaning?	Yes	No
Are the multiple intelligences awakened?	Yes	No
Is there low stress and high enjoyment?	Yes	No
Is there immediate feedback?	Yes	No
Is there active involvement?	Yes	No
Does it provide novelty?	Yes	No

For More Information

- www.yfu-usa.org
- www.nwse.com
- www.afs.org
- *The Exchange Student Survival Kit* by Bettina Hansel

CLASS MEETINGS

Class meetings are when the entire class goes into executive session to make important decisions. The meeting is best run by student officers who have been elected and each student has an opportunity to propose actions, talk for or against proposals, and vote. Class meetings are run by the rules of parliamentary procedure or other established rules, thus ensuring that each person has equal rights and equal opportunities to participate.

Examples of Class Meetings

- A class decides which of several field trips will best serve their learning.

- A class establishes committees to study a current problem and make recommendations.
- A class makes recommendations for future topics of study.
- Some schools use meetings to handle infractions of rules established by the students or school.

Why Use Class Meetings?

- Class meetings are exercises in democracy.
- Students learn how decisions are made and each person's critical role in influencing the outcomes of decisions.
- Students come to better understand fellow students' reasoning and positions.
- Students sharpen critical thinking skills.
- Students learn to organize and present their thoughts.
- Students learn how organizations make decisions.
- Students learn the essentials of parliamentary procedures so that they will feel comfortable and competent in their roles as members of boards and committees in organizations.

Where Would a Teacher Use Class Meetings?

The most common use is in English and social studies classes where the subject matter is about civics, speaking, and correct procedures. Still, this doesn't preclude their use in a less formalistic way in other settings where teachers might not concentrate as much attention on Robert's Rules of Order.

How Does a Teacher Use Class Meetings?

Begin by talking with students about your willingness to share important decisions about future actions. The teacher should be clear about his or her ultimate veto power of decisions that are illegal or inappropriate for the subject matter of the class. Nonetheless, that leaves considerable decision-making capacity for the students as a group. Students will find learning the basics of parliamentary procedure a bit frustrating but that stage doesn't last long and they come to greatly enjoy the

process because there is fair treatment of each person. They need to learn that each person is equal, meaning that each has an equal opportunity to propose ideas, participate in discussion of ideas, and vote on their implementation. The basics of parliamentary procedure include:

- How to make a motion
- Seconding a motion
- Discussion of a motion
- Voting on a motion
- The role of the chairperson or president
- The importance of an accurate record of the proceedings
- The responsibilities of officers and how to select them
- How effective committees are selected and operate

As students learn the basics, they come to relish class meetings. They will ask when the next meeting will occur and rarely will be absent for it. It takes several meetings before this state of mind arrives but it has great payoffs in student morale and learning.

Brain Compatibility: Do You Agree?

Is there emphasis on context and meaning?	Yes	No
Are the multiple intelligences awakened?	Yes	No
Is there low stress and high enjoyment?	Yes	No
Is there immediate feedback?	Yes	No
Is there active involvement?	Yes	No
Does it provide novelty?	Yes	No

For More Information

- www.ncrel.org/sdrs/areas/rpl_esys/collab.htm
- *Class Meetings: Building Leadership, Problem-Solving and Decision-Making Skills in the Respectful Classroom* by Donna Styles
- www.stenhouse.com/pdfs/8134fm.pdf

SPARKS

Sparks is a term devised by Leslie Hart, a pioneer in brain-based learning. He used it to describe activities that create a spark of interest in learning more about a topic. Hart proposed that schools should have several sparks a week. These would be speakers, demonstrations, and events mostly outside the customary activities of the school or class. The old-time school assembly is an example of a spark but has become passé given the power of television to bring lively entertainment into every home. Sparks work best in a smaller setting, say, an individual class or two joined classes, where the give and take permits easy exchanges between the presenter and students.

Examples of Sparks

- A parent explains the nature of her job as an attorney.
- A neighbor tells about a trip to Egypt.
- An artist demonstrates the technique of macramé.
- A city councillor talks to the class via speakerphone.
- An Indian parent tells about her upbringing.

Why Use Sparks?

Sparks add valuable input to the brain, which is often starved for input in the average classroom. The brain needs input. It is the raw material for the basic building blocks of patterns and programs in the brain. The brain is a remarkable pattern-detecting device and will extract meaning from experiences, almost irrespective of their seeming inappropriateness. Sparks provide a new experience for the brain, which is most alert at such times, hence the potential for more learning and new connections to previous learnings.

Where Would a Teacher Use Sparks?

Sparks are appropriate during any class, at any time. Leslie Hart suggested that input to the brain should be increased by 10 times the input found in most classrooms. Sparks provide excellent input.

How Does a Teacher Use Sparks?

Interestingly, almost any kind of spark can be used at any time profitably. Teachers should not worry about whether a given spark will fit the topic under study at the moment. The brain will extract meaning in many ways in response to new sparks. The teacher should be alert to possible sparks. Some poll parents for people willing to share their experiences, for example: careers, hobbies, travels, interests, illnesses, cooking skills, talents, history, and so on. The list is endless. The teacher invites the person to the class (several classes might share the experience), has the person describe his or her interest, and leaves time for interaction with the students.

Brain Compatibility: Do You Agree?

Is there emphasis on context and meaning?	Yes	No
Are the multiple intelligences awakened?	Yes	No
Is there low stress and high enjoyment?	Yes	No
Is there immediate feedback?	Yes	No
Is there active involvement?	Yes	No
Does it provide novelty?	Yes	No

For More Information

- *Human Brain and Human Learning* by L. Hart (1988). Kent, WA: Books for Educators
- "Huge Learning Jumps Show Potency of Brain-Based Instruction" by Charmaine Della Neve, et al., *Phi Delta Kappan*, October 1996

FIELD TRIPS

Field trips are excursions by a class or small group into the community to learn by direct observation or participation. All schools use field trips but few use them extensively because of the expense and other factors. Still, field trips can be used more widely if done in small groups with proper preparation. A search for material on the web turned up endless references to virtual field trips. This discussion focuses on real field trips.

Examples of Field Trips

- A class attends a concert.
- Three students interview the chief of police about delinquency.

- Two students from a math class visit architectural offices to see applications of geometry.

Why Use Field Trips?

Field trips give students firsthand information, an essential way of learning for their brains. Field trips are examples of complex learning because of their many facets. The planning and debriefing of a field trip with students provides valuable reinforcement of learning—crucial knowledge and skills being promoted by a lesson or unit.

Where Would a Teacher Use Field Trips?

Any class benefits from field trips, if properly managed. Teachers can efficiently use field trips more often through small groups.

How Does a Teacher Use Field Trips?

As teachers desire other ways of building understanding, they can turn to the strategy of field trips by thinking about resources in the community. Every community has a gold mine of resources: people, organizations, places, and events. Consider whether it is feasible for the entire class because of cost, supervision, and scheduling. Often, an easier way is to send from two to five students. Costs are less, supervision will be replaced by careful advance planning, and scheduling is a matter of school policy that permits students to miss other classes if on a scheduled field trip. Planning includes a form to parents that describes the trip and informs the parent that the school will not be liable for accidents. Student need to complete forms showing their route, timetable, whom they will meet, where they will meet the resource, and emergency phone information. More important, there must be clarity of purpose; relationship of content to the class; clear, clean questions to gather information about; and, if necessary, rehearsals of how to interview, observe, and take notes.

Finally, students need to do something significant with the experience upon their return. They should prepare a presentation of key points and be prepared to answer questions. They should also review the process of the trip itself: Was the planning adequate? Did transportation arrangements work out? Was the resource helpful? Could students have been better prepared? Did everyone cooperate? These questions add to the learning experience and set the stage for more effective field trips in the future. Figure 4.2 summarizes the planning, execution, and follow-up for a field trip.

Getting Mileage From Field Trips

Before Trip
- Plan with students.
- Have them share what they know already.
- Have them visualize what they will see.
- Make list of questions or things to note.
- Determine significance of trip to their lives.
- Use open-ended probes: On this trip I expect to learn ...
  I'm looking forward to learning ...

During Trip
Review details of the trip:
- How long you will stay?
- Meeting place?
- Lost person?

Have student helpers on the trip:
- Roster keeper
- Photographer
- Note taker
- General assistant
- Introducer
- Thank-you persons

Back Home
Much more is gained from debriefing and reflecting on trip:
- Review what was learned.
- How did the trip compare with what they expected?
- Value of trip?
- Recommend to others?
- Any changes?
- Repeat the trip?
- Related trips?
- Plan follow-up presentations or reports for students who didn't go and for parents.
- Send thank you (students design them, of course).

Figure 4.2.   Getting Mileage From Field Trips

Brain Compatibility: Do You Agree?

Is there emphasis on context and meaning?	Yes	No
Are the multiple intelligences awakened?	Yes	No
Is there low stress and high enjoyment?	Yes	No
Is there immediate feedback?	Yes	No
Is there active involvement?	Yes	No
Does it provide novelty?	Yes	No

For More Information

- www.gsn.org/project/fieldtrips
- *Beyond the Field Trip: Teaching and Learning in Public Places* by Uma Krishnaswami
- See also lists of local places published by the media, chambers of commerce, and so forth.

LEARNED EXPERTISE

Learned expertise is a program in which students become experts at some area of knowledge and subsequently share that knowledge with the teacher or other students.

Examples of Learned Expertise:

- Each student becomes an expert about a state.
- Each student becomes an expert about some career area.
- Pairs of students become experts about a form of literature.

Why Use Learned Expertise?

This strategy motivates students particularly when they have a choice of topic. They enjoy becoming the key person who knows a segment of knowledge and shares it with others. They work hard to gather information on their area and in the process improve in research skills, organizing information, and presentation.

Where Would a Teacher Use Learned Expertise?

Almost any subject with access to information can be used with learned expertise.

How Does a Teacher Use Learned Expertise?

- Tell students that they are going to learn a great deal of information about many aspects about a subject—say, trees.
- Each will choose a tree to investigate and become an expert in information about that tree.
- They will need to gather information from a variety of sources.
- At this point, take time to talk about sources of information: Internet, library, texts, people, organizations, yellow pages, and so on.
- Students then choose their topic and go to work.
- Depending on student skill levels, you may have to teach note taking, interviewing, and data organization.
- It is a good idea to require periodic progress reports, either in writing or orally.
- In a final session, they share their learning with the class, or, better yet, make presentation boards for parents, the public, or other classes to view and make themselves available to respond to questions.

Brain Compatibility: Do You Agree?

Is there emphasis on context and meaning?	Yes	No
Are the multiple intelligences awakened?	Yes	No
Is there low stress and high enjoyment?	Yes	No
Is there immediate feedback?	Yes	No
Is there active involvement?	Yes	No
Does it provide novelty?	Yes	No

For More Information

- *Passion for Learning: How Project-Based Learning Meets the Needs of 21st Century Students* by Ronald Newell

PUPIL-TEACHER PLANNING

Pupil-teacher planning is the practice of planning content and procedures with students. It has been around for a long time, though seldom seen in practice to any major degree. In its pure form, as a means of empowerment, students play major roles in determining the direction and conduct of a class. Few teachers would have the authority or inclination to take it this far, powerful as the strategy is. However, in a more limited way, teachers can very profitably plan aspects of a class with students.

Examples of Pupil-Teacher Planning

* Teachers plan all or most aspects of a field trip *with* students.
* Teachers plan with students what questions the next unit of study in history will address.
* The teacher offers choices of topics in microbiology.

Why Use Pupil-Teacher Planning?

Empowerment of students through shared decision making motivates students. It pays a high compliment to students because the teacher regards their ideas as important. The brain thrives on self-determination and teacher approval. Learning accelerates under conditions of empowerment. Pupil-teacher planning is a form of democracy in action.

Where Would a Teacher Use Pupil-Teacher Planning?

Any class where the teacher wishes to increase learner ownership would be appropriate for pupil-teacher planning.

How Does a Teacher Use Pupil-Teacher Planning?

At its simplest form, offer choices to the class, for example, about which to do first, what topic to do next, or what form of exam to use. The more classic form involves students listing questions they have about a topic or topics. A good way to do this is to have students individually jot down their questions, share these in pairs, list them on the chalkboard, and ultimately vote them up or down after listing criteria for making a decision. The decisions are then implemented, perhaps again involving students in the plans for implementation.

Brain Compatibility: Do You Agree?

Is there emphasis on context and meaning?	Yes	No
Are the multiple intelligences awakened?	Yes	No
Is there low stress and high enjoyment?	Yes	No
Is there immediate feedback?	Yes	No
Is there active involvement?	Yes	No
Does it provide novelty?	Yes	No

For More Information

- "The Situation Made Us Special" by Barbara Brodhagen in *Democratic Schools*, edited by Michael Apple and James Beane
- www.newhorizons.org/strategies/democratic/kennedy.htm
- *Inciting Learning* by Joan Caulfield and Wayne Jennings

DAILY NEWSPAPER

The daily newspaper strategy uses the community newspaper in the classroom for extending and amplifying learning.

Examples of the Daily Newspaper Strategy

- Students present items from the newspaper in civics twice a week.
- Students in math class determine batting averages and compare their numbers with statistics from the sports page.
- Students in science examine the weather page for interesting climatic data.
- Students use the *Wall Street Journal* to study ideas about economic policy.

Why Use the Daily Newspaper Strategy?

The newspaper reports on reality, thus linking school to the real world. This adds meaning that reinforces and deepens learning. Students may even talk with parents about their newspaper and its connection to school learning. Students take a greater interest in the newspaper and discover many interesting parts to major newspapers. With this knowledge, schoolwork comes more alive and its relevance can be seen.

Where Would a Teacher Use the Daily Newspaper Strategy?

Any class can apply the newspaper as a teaching/learning tool.

How Does a Teacher Use the Daily Newspaper Strategy?

The school should subscribe to a bundle of newspapers. These can be divided among classes or shared on certain days. Most newspaper publishers make classroom sets available at a substantial discount. Students on a rotating basis can be given assignments every day to report on relevant topics, from sports, political cartoons, and statistics to science in the news, funnies (don't forget humor in the classroom), want ads, and so forth. These offer opportunities for discussion, questions, follow-up, reflection—all resulting in more learning. Some newspapers publish booklets of, say, 100 ways to use the newspaper in the classroom.

Brain Compatibility: Do You Agree?

Is there emphasis on context and meaning?	Yes	No
Are the multiple intelligences awakened?	Yes	No
Is there low stress and high enjoyment?	Yes	No
Is there immediate feedback?	Yes	No
Is there active involvement?	Yes	No
Does it provide novelty?	Yes	No

For More Information

- www.suelebeau.com/nie.htm
- www.cnnstudentnews.cnn.com/fyi/
- www.eduref.org/cgi-bin/printlessons.cgi/Virtual/Lessons/Language_Arts/Journalism/JNL0199.html
- Check with your large city newspaper publishers for booklets on using the newspapers in classes.

EXHIBITIONS AND PRESENTATIONS

Exhibitions and presentations offer students a chance to show what they
have learned in a public setting, either in the classroom for peers or in
a broader community setting. Students give presentations about a completed project or on what they have researched. They may do this in
many ways: storyboards, media presentations, drama, speeches, public
displays, and so on.

Examples of Exhibitions and Presentations

- Students set up science-fair types of displays at the mall for the
  public to view.
- As a culminating activity, students present their future schools projects to another class.
- Students present a skit to the city council on the need for a youth
  recreation center.
- Students make presentations to other classes or at nearby elementary schools.

Why Use Exhibitions and Presentations?

An exhibition of learning for an audience beyond the teacher motivates students to higher levels of performance. The last thing a student
wants is to look foolish. The brain prefers active learning and opportunities to test its powers by demonstrating skills and knowledge.

Where Would a Teacher Use Exhibitions and Presentations?

Any class is a perfect setting for exhibitions and presentations as a culminating activity.

How Does a Teacher Use Exhibitions and Presentations?

The teacher informs the class that the culmination of a topic will be
via an exhibition or presentation, preferably in a public venue, and establishes a firm date. Students will summarize what they learned via the

exhibit or demonstration in lieu of an exam. Students either work individually or in teams to learn the material and then find creative ways to present their work. The teacher becomes a valuable resource person to the individual students or teams.

Brain Compatibility: Do You Agree?

Is there emphasis on context and meaning?	Yes	No
Are the multiple intelligences awakened?	Yes	No
Is there low stress and high enjoyment?	Yes	No
Is there immediate feedback?	Yes	No
Is there active involvement?	Yes	No
Does it provide novelty?	Yes	No

For More Information

- www.essentialschools.org/cs/resources/view/ces_res/138
- *Passion for Learning: How Project-Based Learning Meets the Needs of 21st Century Students* by Ronald Newell
- www.essentialschools.org/cs/resources/view/ces_res/136

ENTREPRENEURSHIP

Entrepreneurship in a secondary school setting is when students run a real business with a product or service, generally intended to produce a profit.

Examples of Entrepreneurship

- Students operate a school store as part of a class.
- Students start and operate a business making name badges.
- Students obtain contracts with small businesses to do graphic designing for ads and placards.
- Students operate an ethnic restaurant for staff or neighbors.

Why Use Entrepreneurship?

Students learn important skills and knowledge, such as making a business plan, determining markup for a product, keeping books, salesmanship, and principles of economics. In the process, students use reading, writing, and arithmetic skills. Entrepreneurship programs generate enthusiasm and energy, which means student brains are alive and receptive. Entrepreneurship brings reality to school lessons to deepen learning.

Where Would a Teacher Use Entrepreneurship?

At a simple level, any teacher might use a form of entrepreneurship by involving students in a fund-raising activity, such as selling cupcakes or a car wash. At a more serious level, social studies, math, industrial technology, and business education teachers could justify involving students in forming and operating a business.

How Does a Teacher Use Entrepreneurship?

While entrepreneurship units come up as a part of some programs, a more motivating process would involve discussions with students about operating a business, visits to other programs with entrepreneurship units, talks by community resource businesspeople (don't forget diversity here), brainstorming about possible products or services, outlining the steps necessary to begin a business, selecting teams for the various tasks, and implementing plans. It is valuable to have frequent progress reports to discuss issues and problems so that classmates can learn from one another and offer suggestions. Equally important are debriefing and reflection as the businesses get underway and at the completion of the program.

Brain Compatibility: Do You Agree?		
Is there emphasis on context and meaning?	Yes	No
Are the multiple intelligences awakened?	Yes	No
Is there low stress and high enjoyment?	Yes	No
Is there immediate feedback?	Yes	No
Is there active involvement?	Yes	No
Does it provide novelty?	Yes	No

For More Information

- www.ye.entreworld.org/
- www.edtecinc.com/edu_prods_nye.htm
- www.nfte.com/contact/

ORAL HISTORY

Oral history is having students tap into the knowledge and activities of people in the community through a process of recording information for future use.

Examples of Oral History

- Students write stories and take photographs, as in the *Foxfire* magazine project.
- Students interview senior citizens about their lives.
- Students publish a book of poetry by local residents.

Why Use Oral History?

Important skills of interviewing, note taking, summarizing information, meeting people and having them feel at ease, photographing, writing, rewriting, and publishing are learned in the context of a real task of interest to students. Learning about real people and their lives is of high interest to students. Accordingly, student brains are at their most receptive and learning is deeper and more permanent.

Where Would a Teacher Use Oral History?

Any subject is suitable, but perhaps most appropriately in English or social studies. Programs using interdisciplinary approaches also benefit from the strategy.

How Does a Teacher Use Oral History?

A teacher might start by asking students what questions they have about people and activities in the community. This can be followed up by asking how students might best get answers to these questions. The teacher can suggest that the direct approach of talking with people, recording their remarks accurately, and sharing their findings with a broader audience would be an exciting and effective learning experience. Many skills would be learned so that students could approach the task with confidence and professional competence.

Brain Compatibility: Do You Agree?

Is there emphasis on context and meaning?	Yes	No
Are the multiple intelligences awakened?	Yes	No
Is there low stress and high enjoyment?	Yes	No
Is there immediate feedback?	Yes	No
Is there active involvement?	Yes	No
Does it provide novelty?	Yes	No

For More Information

- www.foxfire.org/teachi.htm
- www.historymatters.gmu.edu/mse/oral
- www.library.ucsc.edu/reg-hist/ohprimer.html

VIDEOTAPING

Videotaping is using the power of television to capture an event for analysis or future presentation. Television equipment for the school or classroom has become far less expensive and is simpler to use and edit than in the past.

Examples of Videotaping

- A coach has students videotape other students in gymnastics to perfect moves.
- Students videotape elder citizens about their experiences in the armed services.
- Students videotape a skit to use as part of presentations over community video channels.

Why Use Videotaping?

Videotaping offers many experiences to exercise executive skills, such as decisions about who, what, when and where to tape; editing for best effects; editing for content; the importance of accuracy and fairness; and perfecting skills and routines. Students greatly enjoy videotaping and its links to their own television viewing habits.

Where Would a Teacher Use Videotaping?

Any teacher sending students out to gather information can use videotaping as a way of capturing the information and using the intrinsic motivation students have about being given an important real assignment, using equipment, and viewing television. Videotaping can be used within the classroom and school to prepare presentations of information.

How Does a Teacher Use Videotaping?

A school needs to obtain basic equipment such as handheld cameras, editing machines or editing software, and either videotape players or CD players. Most schools have at least some of this equipment at present or it can be obtained for a fairly modest cost. The manuals for the equipment provide helpful hints on how to use it. Some schools have contacted a local college for the use of one of their students in a video program to help students get started. Students also need instruction on the care of equipment. The teacher can be alert to situations that would benefit from videotaping. Once students get started with videotaping, they will be eager to use their skills of videotaping and editing. Editing, writing a script, practicing a presentation, and sharing the results with an audience follow the actual interviewing and videotaping.

Brain Compatibility: Do You Agree?

Is there emphasis on context and meaning?	Yes	No
Are the multiple intelligences awakened?	Yes	No
Is there low stress and high enjoyment?	Yes	No
Is there immediate feedback?	Yes	No
Is there active involvement?	Yes	No
Does it provide novelty?	Yes	No

For More Information

- www.angelfire.com/ar2/videomanual1
- www.cecsep.usu.edu/resources/vcresources/vcvideotaping.htm

- *303 Digital Filmmaking Solutions : Solve Any Video Shoot or Edit Problem in Ten Minutes or Less, for Ten Dollars or Less* by Chuck B. Gloman

GAMES

A game is an activity involving a playful situation in which students compete (and sometimes cooperate) in order to win. Games are simulations that students respond to with excitement and energy.

Examples of Games

- Students play Jeopardy about historical information.
- Student teams compete for best scores on informal exams in science.
- Student "expert" panel responds to questions from the class in culture studies.

Why Use Games?

Students enjoy games because they bring amusement and fun into drab, humdrum school lives. During games, student minds are alive and alert, thus more learning of various kinds occurs. Students receive praise and encouragement from fellow team members, always a valuable practice.

Where Would a Teacher Use Games?

Any class, any subject can use games to spark interest and enthusiasm.

How Does a Teacher Use Games?

Students are pretty good at making up games so a teacher might ask if there is any way to make a game out of learning the material. Teachers can use popular television programs as a format for the game. Teachers can use the material scheduled for review or examination as game content and as an alternative process of preparing for an exam.

Brain Compatibility: Do You Agree?

Is there emphasis on context and meaning?	Yes	No
Are the multiple intelligences awakened?	Yes	No
Is there low stress and high enjoyment?	Yes	No
Is there immediate feedback?	Yes	No
Is there active involvement?	Yes	No
Does it provide novelty?	Yes	No

For More Information

- *Design Your Own Games and Activities: Thiagi's Templates for Performance Improvement* by Sivasailam Thiagarajan
- www.nova.edu/~spahn/games_for_learning.html
- www.webtools.cityu.edu.hk/news/newslett/learningwithrole.htm

PROJECT-BASED LEARNING

Students work individually or in groups on a project of their choosing or as assigned by the teacher.

Examples of Project-Based/Problem-Based Learning

- A student researches car engines for displacement.
- Several students work together to catalog the animals at the zoo.
- Students explore careers in aviation.

Why Use Project-Based/Problem-Based Learning?

Project-based learning supports differentiated instruction. When student choose projects or problems to investigate, motivation and quality of work soar. Teachers can change from sage to facilitator.

Where Would a Teacher Use Project-Based/Problem-Based Learning?

Any class after students learn the skills of researching, organizing information, and presenting their findings would be appropriate for this strategy.

How Does a Teacher Use Project-Based/Problem-Based Learning?

- Students state their project in the form of a question or goal with a timeline for completion.
- Students cite at least three sources of information on the topic (Internet, books, films, people, etc.).
- Students search for information from these sources on their topic.
- Students record their findings.
- Students organize their findings.
- Students devise creative ways to present their information.
- Students and teacher determine how the project will be evaluated.
- Students reflect on what they learned and the process of learning.

Brain Compatibility: Do You Agree?

Is there emphasis on context and meaning?	Yes	No
Are the multiple intelligences awakened?	Yes	No
Is there low stress and high enjoyment?	Yes	No
Is there immediate feedback?	Yes	No
Is there active involvement?	Yes	No
Does it provide novelty?	Yes	No

For More Information

- *Passion for Learning: How Project-Based Learning Meets the Needs of 21st Century Students* by Ronald Newell
- http://glef.org/PBL/howpbl.html
- www.pblmm.k12.ca.us/PBLGuide/WhyPBL.html

RETROSPECTIVE

Retrospective refers to studying an experience gained earlier by others to gain perspective about something new. Retrospective is a special type of reflection, itself a powerful strategy.

Examples of Retrospective:

- Graduates return to their former school to share their reflections with students or faculty.

- Students offer advice at the end of the year in individual letters to the students who will sit in their classroom seats.
- Dropouts explain to teachers—or fellow students—why they left school.

Why Use Retrospective?

The unique first-person perspective gained from an experience that others might repeat provides valuable information to the new candidate. Learners gain a sense of what it is like to "walk in another's shoes." The brain desires feedback in order to do its best and the experience of another is instructive. At such a stage, the brain is uniquely open to information. The person presenting the retrospective engages in a rigorous process of thinking, reflection, and organizing his or her thoughts.

Where Would a Teacher Use Retrospective?

Any situation where learners encounter a new situation and could profit from the experience of their predecessors is suitable for retrospection.

How Does a Teacher Use Retrospective?

- One teacher asked students to reflect on the school year and to put their thoughts in a letter of advice to the student who would occupy their desk in the coming year. Students were to suggest ways for the incoming student to be more successful in that class.
- A school staff paid rapt attention as six students in the school told their story of what led to drug addiction and their excruciating attempts at reclaiming their lives.
- Inviting previous graduates to tell of their experiences in school provides valuable insights about how the program met student needs and prepared them for the next stage of their lives. The same presentation to students will be particularly meaningful because of a role-model effect.

Brain Compatibility: Do You Agree?

Is there emphasis on context and meaning?	Yes	No
Are the multiple intelligences awakened?	Yes	No
Is there low stress and high enjoyment?	Yes	No
Is there immediate feedback?	Yes	No
Is there active involvement?	Yes	No
Does it provide novelty?	Yes	No

For More Information

- www.infed.org/foundations/w-inf4.htm
- www.unca.edu/et/br022102.html
- www.studentsinservicetoamerica.org/tools_resources/docs/nwtool kit.pdf

5

SHOWCASE OF POWERFUL PRACTICES FROM TEACHERS IN THEIR OWN WORDS

In this chapter, we offer additional strategies to stimulate your thinking and reinforce your own good practice. Teachers sent these to us. These strategies range on a continuum from those that can be used in any school setting to those that can be only undertaken in more innovative, bolder settings. Some might not seem feasible for you. Still, don't be too quick to discard an idea; you may be able to tweak an idea to work for you. Every one of these practices began when a teacher took a chance and went for the gold. You may be more ready to prospect than you think! And now we proudly present . . . bonus brain-compatible strategies for your consideration from teachers in their own words and format.

TOWN BLITZ BY BERTRAND FIELDS

My students and I decided to study a small town by learning as much as we possibly could and understanding as deeply as possible all aspects of the town. We decided to select a town about one hour's bus ride away. We drew a circle on a map and selected a small town, Northfield, that had two private colleges within its boundaries.

We made plans to visit the town in about a month so that we would
have time to study and research the town in advance of our visit. We began by brainstorming sources of information using a software program
called Inspiration, as seen in Figure 5.1. We then decided on what items
to pursue and divided into teams to gather as much background about
the town as we could find.

We contacted the local newspapers for back and current issues, the
Northfield Chamber of Commerce for their promotional literature, the
city hall and the mayor's office, both colleges for promotional materials,
and, of course, checked the Internet, which led to sources we didn't

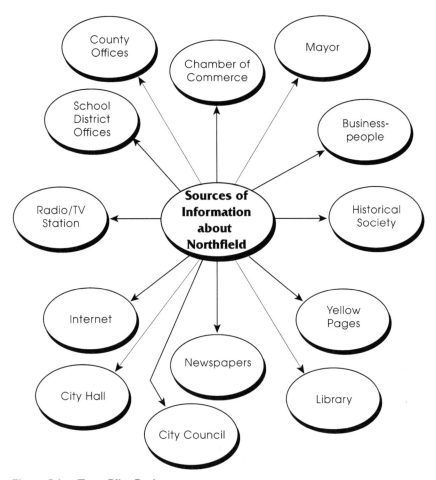

Figure 5.1.   Town Blitz Brainstorm

expect—namely, real estate agents who introduced us to the various neighborhoods of the town and their relative merits.

When word got out about our study, a couple of unusual things happened. Two people called us to say they had once lived in Northfield but now lived in our present city and were excited to tell us about their life in Northfield. Interestingly, their views differed—one had warm feelings about the town and the other was somewhat negative, with complaints about the "rowdy" college students.

We learned about several controversies brewing in the community. One had to do with a school referendum to raise money and the other with zoning laws involving commercial expansion of a business. I was surprised how quickly my students learned about these issues that were not part of their previous knowledge and experience base.

Every day, there was new information and revelations to share. Excitement built with students eager to see and experience the town directly beyond the vicarious level. We decided to divide the class into teams for the actual trip. Teams consisted of two to four students each. Each team would have two assignments when we arrived at the town. These included such items as interviews of the mayor, newspaper editor, police chief, school superintendent, high school principal, real estate agent, or several businesspeople; and visits or tours of the colleges, several businesses, a small park, or the downtown area. I gave mini-lessons on how to conduct research, handle interviews, take notes, write letters, make phone calls, and other skills needed for the trip. We role-played a number of the activities to refine skills.

On the day of the trip, we spread across town to gather information. At noon, we gathered near the river that ran through the middle of the town for a picnic lunch and to share ideas. Several students had special assignments: food, photography, videotaping, making sketches, writing thank-you notes. We returned having felt it was a very good day.

We spent the next several days preparing summaries, charts, and exhibitions for others, including parents, to see. I agreed with the students who said they had learned a great deal and we filled the chalkboard with a list of the skills and knowledge we had gained. Several students wrote descriptions about the trip, the town, the people they met; one student wrote a poem, several made drawings, and another wrote a song.

The enthusiasm of the students for the town blitz was clearly evident because they said that this type of study had been our best project of the year and they hoped there would be more of such activities in their future classes.

THE FOUR CORNERS BY MAXINE GARRISON

For our middle school students, four is the magic number. Over the course of the year, we focus on four overarching sets of skills: reading, writing, listening and speaking, and information literacy. Small groups often consist of four students. We utilize the four-square method to plan our writing activities (Gould & Gould, 2002).

At the core of our brain-based approach to instruction and learning, we also use a couple of strategies emphasizing four: a four-corners activity and a menu of four activity options. The four-corners activity is utilized as a way to stimulate thinking and encourage active participation in the classroom and can be used at any grade level with any subject.

We often assess or extend our thinking, reading, and writing with a choice of four activity options as a way to monitor and extend student learning. The four-corners activity and the four activity options are highlights in our classroom instruction, which is heavily influenced by brain-based theories and practice.

Four corners is a strategy that facilitates a constructivist approach to learning with a strong focus on creating meaning. The subsequent benefit of this is a higher probability of students not only remembering but also using the concepts and ideas discussed.

The strategy encourages mental and physical participation by everyone, yet the environment is safe due to the element of choice and the awareness of there being no right answer. To me, this is a critical component of the strategy. Students who do not feel safe are not going to be fully engaged, willing, or able to focus enough for the complex thinking the activity requires. The choice and movement inherent in four corners gives them multiple ways to participate—alone if they feel secure enough and together if they do not.

Cognitively, four corners is a win-win setting. Students have to think before they make a choice, they have to listen to others and integrate that information with their own knowledge, and then they evaluate whether or not to make a change. I've found that the beauty of the activity is that students get so involved in it that metacognition happens naturally. They don't have to be persuaded or reminded to think critically.

In terms of instruction, the strategy takes almost no preparation time or materials, and, even better, gives inside information as to how students are thinking and from what perspectives. It's a free look into their world.

The following will show you how to use four corners for various purposes. Please keep in mind that this strategy is extremely flexible with virtually unlimited uses and adaptations.

1. *Use with thematic discussion: "Harrison Bergeron" by Kurt Vonnegut.* This particular short story is a great one for teaching theme because it has multiple possibilities with an abundance of story support for each one. After ensuring literal comprehension of the story, I write four possible themes and place one in each corner of the room. For example, I might have:
   • Be careful what you wish for.
   • Without diversity, there can be no progress.
   • Force should never be used to ensure equality.
   • Equity and equality are not the same.
   Students decide which theme they feel the story best supports and stand in that corner. Undecided students stand in the middle. Then, students are asked to justify their choice with specific support from the story. No one in a different corner is allowed to talk at this time. When all corners have been heard from, students are given a chance to change their theme choice, and the undecided students in the middle must choose a theme. Everyone is in a corner at this point. Students who chose for the first time or changed positions now explain their move.

   I have also put the traditional four corner signs—agree, strongly agree, disagree, and strongly disagree—in the corners and have had students choose one after I state a theme. They then complete the same process of support and change. An additional idea for literary discussion would be to put character traits in the corners, assign students different characters, and have them stand under the traits that fit best. Again, they would have to justify their choice by character actions and speech in the story. A statement could be made about a character or a prediction could be stated and the agree/disagree signs could be used for that as well.

2. *Use in diversity instruction.* Simply place the Agree and Disagree signs in the room. Make a statement and have students stand under the sign that best fits their opinion. Follow the same process used for the literature discussions.

   With diversity instruction, I make commonly assumed statements about welfare, homelessness, crime, and so forth. After students have gone through the decision and justification process, I read the fact that disproves the misconception, and give them a chance to discuss the prejudices that caused the initial statement. The contrast between the preconceived notion and the fact really gets their attention. It also allows for discussion of possible reasons behind the misconception.

   Note: Be prepared for students to divulge personal information when you do this. I was amazed how many kids came forward with personal poverty and welfare experiences when a generalization was stated about welfare use. I would not have guessed the background of some of these kids.

3. *Use with debatable topics.* Four corners can be used for almost anything that needs to be discussed, even classroom and behavioral issues. If the topic is relevant to the grade level and student population, it will be an effective option. Here are a few I've used to generate diversity and social climate discussion.

   • The only official language in this country should be English.
   • The use of Native American mascots and names for team sports are all in the name of fun and do not really harm people. In fact, they could be perceived as a compliment.
   • There is no longer a significant problem with prejudice in our society.

4. *Use with writing.* As one might expect, four corners can be used a number of ways with writing as well. It can enhance prewriting by generating ideas and discussion of topics, or be used after writing as a way to share. A student can state the thesis of his or her work,

and other students can agree/disagree with it. After hearing responses, the writer can then give his or her justifications. It can also be used during the revision stage of the writing process with the strategy implemented after the first draft with younger students and the second draft with older, more accomplished writers.

FOUR ACTIVITY OPTIONS BY MELISSA TAYLOR

I began to develop and use the four activity options as I was struggling to incorporate differentiation, Bloom's Taxonomy, and Gardner's notion of multiple intelligences into my classroom. These menus offer students a choice of four activities that demonstrate understanding of a lesson and extend that understanding in meaningful, creative ways that encourage higher-level thinking and the utilization of different cognitive skills. I generally develop at least one menu for every unit of instruction.

Students appreciate having the ability to choose how to demonstrate their learning on a regular basis and, because they cannot choose the same type of activity repeatedly, I enjoy seeing them develop different skills and abilities.

This use of menus is not new to the classroom. Many talented teachers have created various types of project options for their students. But what I like about my four-activity options is its simplicity and focus. Creating four choices is much easier than creating a tic-tac-toe with nine choices, and I believe that my planned choices of activities allow me to assess my students on various abilities while providing them with meaningful, fun options to demonstrate their learning.

Creating the menus is easy. I simply decide how I want to use the activities—as a means to assess learning or as a means to extend it. Then, I think of four different types of activities for the students. These are inserted into squares labeled A, B, C, D:

A. An application-level activity
B. A synthesis-level activity that involves writing
C. A creative or artistic project
D. A comprehension- or evaluation-level activity

The different types of activities are placed in the same square. For ex-ample, the artistic or creative projects are in a square labeled "C." Stu-dents cannot repeat a letter until they have done each type of project at least once. They enjoy challenging their traditional ways of thinking, and I enjoy evaluating their products. Here is an example of a way to use this strategy.

Editorial Writing

The four activity options have worked well to extend students' writing activities. Often, students focus on producing a substantial piece of writ-ing, only to forget about it the minute it is handed in to the teacher. One of the substantial pieces of writing that our students are expected to write is an editorial. The four corners activity stimulates their thinking about debatable issues. For example, after reading *The House of Scor-pion* by Nancy Farmer (an excellent young adult novel about a clone) and various scientific articles about cloning in science class, students de-cide if cloning should be illegal in every case, legal for research pur-poses, legal for animal use, or legal for any purpose, including human cloning for individual benefit. After choosing a corner and debating the issue as a class, students begin to understand the complexity of issues and are ready to brainstorm topics for their editorials. After completing the writing process on the editorials, students choose one of the activity options listed below.

1. Publish your editorial in a local newspaper. Select a paper that will be interested in your topic, research how to send in your writing, and revise and edit carefully. In a brief paper (less than one page), explain how you chose a newspaper and how you revised your ed-itorial for your new, broader audience. Editorials must focus on a debatable topic. Rewrite your editorial in a "different" voice. For example, if you were in favor of your focus issue, write an editorial against that issue.
2. Find three recent editorial cartoons. Analyze how the artists talk about a major issue in only a drawing and caption. Write about your analysis in a paragraph. Draw an original editorial cartoon fo-cusing on your issue.

3. Find one administrator or politician who does not share your view of your editorial issue. Write a letter to that person explaining your viewpoint. You may wish to include a copy of your editorial. Encourage that person to respond to you.

Using Activity Options With a Novel

The idea to utilize activity options with a novel comes from Janet Allen. She referred to her activity as a Four Square for Fiction and included activities that allowed students to display comprehension of the novel using various reading strategies. We recently completed this type of activity option as we read *The Well* by Mildred Taylor. At various points in the book, students would complete a square of their choice so that students completed all squares. Activity options include:

1. Summarize three or four of the main events from our reading so far. Be specific. Use details and names.
2. Visualize a scene, item, or picture from the reading. Draw what you pictured in your head.
3. Connect something from this book to another book you've read or to a societal issue or event. Use details to explain your connection.
4. Contrast Paul-Edward and Old Man McCalister Simms as fathers in a graphic organizer. Who would you rather have for a dad? Support your answer with details from the story.

Possibilities for the activity options are limitless. In my classroom, they have almost completely replaced traditional worksheets. Students have responded well to the change. The environment in my classroom is much more collaborative because the students appreciate having choices, and appreciate the opportunity to direct their own learning. Students must also constantly evaluate their abilities. If they choose a simple comprehension activity for setting, they know that they will have to produce something at a higher level for the next literary element that we study. Often, they will reserve the lower-level activities as a final option. Including this simple element of choice in a framework that incorporates Bloom's Taxonomy and Gardner's multiple intelligences has increased student interest, participation, and motivation.

INTEREST-BASED LEARNING BY BILL ZIMNIEWICZ

At an alternative school for at-risk students, students complete personal learning plans (see Chapter 4, Learning Strategies) with particularly strong emphasis on their interests. Students are expected to pursue topics and subjects of interest. Teachers probe students who say they have no interests to discover what interests them. It always turns out that there are interests. Sometimes students interpret a question about their interests as related to school subjects. That's why the teacher-advisors confer with students to learn of interests beyond school.

For example, it was found that a student without any stated interests wanted to have the city build a skateboarding area in the park. The teacher channeled the student's interest through a series of questions to investigate:

- What is a skateboarding area?
- How much space does it take?
- What is a good design for a skateboarding area?
- What would it cost?
- Who else is interested in skateboard ramps?
- Who makes decisions about public recreational areas?

Each of these would take time and skills to research and to find information. Ultimately there were many other questions. The student was particularly interested in the design of skateboard ramps but recognized the importance of the other initial questions and many others as the project progressed. The student who had been listless and disengaged in school became driven to learn about all aspects of skateboarding.

In fact, the skateboarding project became the entire curriculum for virtually the whole day for the student. Teachers became true facilitators of learning in advising the student on how to find information, such as who manufactured skateboards and where to find information on designs for skateboarding ramps. Teachers were valuable resource people, as the student needed help with research, writing, interviewing, speaking, taking notes, reading, math, and art during various phases of the student's project.

The student built a model, created a project board, and gave presentations on his project. On another occasion, two students or a team might have worked on this project, though this particular student chose to work alone. A project of this complexity could have involved a task force of students to pursue all facets.

On another occasion, students might have pursued a course of community decision making to mount support for a skateboarding park. This might have taken such directions as public versus private funding, seeking support of public officials, working with architects and designers, participating in the actual construction, and trips to other existing skateboarding parks to learn how they came about.

Project-based learning can be an entire curriculum, as it is at this alternative school for its students. Other students chose such topics as fighter planes, abortion, motorcycles, sound systems, cosmetology, or Mexican foods—the topics of interest to youth are endless. One student wrote a novel about her own life.

On the other hand, project-based learning can take place within a single subject by permitting students to choose topics of the unit under study. For example, in a social studies unit on westward expansion, the teacher might offer a considerable menu of topics for individual or group projects, such as railroads, Indians, ranching, battles, clothing, hardships, leadership, and prairies. Giving students choice taps motivation.

DEVELOPING STUDENT VOICE IN WRITING BY AMY REILLY

What is a writer's voice? It comes from the emotions of the writer. It lends originality to writing and allows the personality of the writer to shine through. It is confident, enthusiastic, and very diverse. A strong writer's voice can show a wide range of emotions—from humor and joy to anger and sadness.

A strong writer's voice should show that the writer writes honestly and from the heart. It is evident to the reader that the author feels strongly about what has been written.

How does one help students write with a strong voice? The best advice is tell them to be themselves, to look at the topic from several different angles, to choose the one with which they are most comfortable, and to remember that voice changes with your audience. For example, the way you would tell your friends that you flunked a test is much different from the way you would tell your parents.

The best way to help students find their writing voices is to have them practice, practice, practice. A few fun activities to get things started are:

- Who am I?
- Students can choose an inanimate object and write from that object's perspective. For instance, students can write from the perspective of a tooth in their mouth, the sidewalk on which they travel to and from school, or a tire that has gone flat. The possibilities are endless.
- Design a speech for a celebrity or famous person.
- Write about a time in which they felt very wronged. After completing it, they must write about the same situation from the point of view of the person who wronged them.
- Students listen to a piece of music and write the way the music makes them feel. They could also come up with possible places or scenarios in which the music might be played.
- Put a wide variety of well-known characters into a hat. Have students pick from the hat and retell a story from the character's perspective (U.S. president, a rap star, Shaquille O'Neal, Bill Gates, a brain surgeon, etc.).

PARENT-EMPOWERED MATH TUTORING BY DR. HOWARD MYERS

By the time freshmen come to us, the accumulation of math material that is poorly learned or not learned at all can seem overwhelming. Success in math has been elusive, perhaps because of an infamous bugaboo: math phobia among most parents and many teachers.

Our perennial dilemma in math is how to repeat elementary and middle school (or even how to do it for the first time) and still stay on track with high school requirements. The default solution is multifocused classrooms, spanning several levels in a single day to dual-track elementary grades along with high school. Many classes resemble a building site where a contractor on a tight deadline is rushing to build walls, roof, and foundation—all at the same time. It is often a struggle, and certainly not a model solution for everybody. Even in the best years we can't be fully satisfied.

We are always seeking effective ways to address educational deficits from earlier grades, particularly in math. Our math teachers now spend after-school time prepping 11th graders for their high-stakes exam. In addition, a new program of after-school tutoring for 9th and 10th grades focuses on a very basic set of remedial skills in both math and reading. Like elementary school, tutoring centers on the student rather than a particular subject.

In addition to an expanded range of teachers, we are also recruiting parents to tutor their students. A key innovation allows not only non-math specialists but even nonteachers as well to be confident using the tutoring material. This is because basic topics are posted on our website and linked to interactive web pages, now accessible to anyone with an Internet connection. Whether teacher or parent, each tutor acts primarily as guide and audience. He or she gets students to the right web page, and then helps them to read the directions and understand the problem. A final and key role for the tutor is to encourage the student to stay on task.

This approach works well for us because most of our students are computer literate. All 9th-grade students receive a technology orientation course, and our school's ratio of students to Internet-connected computers is 2:1. And although 60–80 percent meet federal criteria for low student-family income, many have Internet access at home.

Thus, students are well prepared for a learning context in which *the web page is often the teacher*. The website typically asks content questions, signals immediately whether a student's response is correct or not, and in some cases provides an explanation. Students are quite used to this format, which often resembles a video game. Our parents are also being introduced to the new approach in a series of evening meetings and their response has been enthusiastic.

In essence, a web-based format empowers parents and other nonmath specialists to guide students to specific tutorial sites. The content outline, summarized below, emphasizes carefully chosen elementary-level math and reading topics that are some of the most frequent stumbling blocks in our high school math program. To view the full program with interactive websites supporting each topic, go to www.essextech.org, then click on "Parent Resources," and then on "Math Guide."

Top Ten Keys to Math Literacy

Welcome—How to Use This Website
Entry Level—First Five Keys
   1. Checkbook math
   2. Credit card math
   3. Fractions and measurement
   4. Tables and graphs
   5. Reading for problem solving
The Next Level—Five More Keys
   6. Area and perimeter
   7. Ratio
   8. Proportion
   9. Percent
   10. Fractions and conversions

For the majority of our students, even the first five entry-level topics can be difficult to master. These topics are the primary focus of tutoring and particularly of parent-led remediation. The welcome page and topic headings are designed to maximize accessibility and deflect math phobia. In the web material and in training workshops, parents and non-math teachers are repeatedly reassured.

The entry-level topics are just what you do to manage your checkbook and credit card, shop for discounts, or use a ruler. You find tables of information and graphs in the newspaper, in work schedules, and in job-related documents. Solving problems, in all sorts of variations, is something we all do.

The website outlined above is also the core of our after-school tutoring program for 9th and 10th grades. With our teachers, however, we add appropriate reading and language arts materials. These are chosen by subject specialists to link with and support the math fundamentals. So far, it all seems to be working as intended. Parents are getting involved, students are beginning the tutoring process, and some math teachers are beginning to see links to their daytime classes.

Today's high school math program is a major challenge for many students. But the answer is not simply to scrap new material or dumb down the curriculum. All students need substantive mathematics, so instructional delivery must accommodate a greater diversity of learners and address a wider range of learning styles.

But improved teaching is only part of the full solution. Ultimately, high school students must command and apply a key set of elementary-level concepts and skills. Students can flounder in today's high school waters if they are without a solid grasp of math fundamentals. In the many cases where students have not mastered elementary concepts before high school, this gap demands effective remediation. Can we expect the school and its math teachers to shoulder the full burden? The value of reading to children and discussing ideas with them is widely recognized, but where is the parallel focus in basic math? To the extent that parents and the school community may have abdicated an active role in addressing many student learning gaps, it seems time to step up. For these and other nonspecialists, web-based math tutoring represents a potential new path to effective action.

EYE ON THE NEWS BY CATHY POLANSKY

Objectives

1. To increase awareness of how fairly newscasts represent all segments of the population.
2. To offer feedback to a local television station regarding their inclusivity and fair depiction of people.

The purpose of this exercise is to give the students an opportunity to critically view the daily news, checking for fair representation and inclusivity of groups. The students study the news, fill out a report card (such as Figure 5.2) for that station, and mail it to the station. Ideally, news broadcasts will be viewed over the span of a week or two. It's best to form a partnership with a local channel that furnishes the broadcasts and meet with students to explain how news decisions are made.

TV News Report Card

TODAY'S DATE _____

FROM _____ DATE OF NEWSCAST _____

SCHOOL _____ TIME OF NEWSCAST _____

STREET ADDRESS _____

CITY _____ STATE _____ZIP _____

RE: Our report card on the inclusivity and fairness of your TV broadcast.

We rated your TV broadcast on your efforts of inclusivity and fairness in representing all diverse communities in a nonstereotypical light. We live in a diverse community and appreciate it when the media takes the time to be representative of our varied communities. Here is our report card and some suggestions for improvement. A is the highest rating.

Inclusivity		Fair Representation	
African Americans	A B C D E F	African Americans	A B C D E F
Asian Americans	A B C D E F	Asian Americans	A B C D E F
European Americans	A B C D E F	European Americans	A B C D E F
Native Americans	A B C D E F	Native Americans	A B C D E F
Hispanic/Latino Amer.	A B C D E F	Hispanic/Latino Amer.	A B C D E F
Men	A B C D E F	Men	A B C D E F
Women	A B C D E F	Women	A B C D E F
People with Disabilities	A B C D E F	People with Disabilities	A B C D E F
Young People	A B C D E F	Young People	A B C D E F
Senior Citizens	A B C D E F	Senior Citizens	A B C D E F

Suggestions for inclusivity:

Figure 5.2. TV News Report Card

Directions

- Ask the students if they watch the evening news. Have them list the things they usually see on the news. List these on the board in broad categories.
- Ask the purpose of the news.
- State that today we are going to watch taped newscasts from a local station. Our goal is for us to rate the newscast on how well they represent the community in which we live.

- Ask students how well they think the news does in fairly representing various groups in our community (for example, African Americans, Asian Americans, European Americans, Native Americans, Hispanic/Latino Americans, men, women, people with disabilities, young people, senior citizens, or others) equitably in both a positive and negative light? Get a general consensus of a grade from the class, A through F.
- Distribute the "TV News Report Card" to each student. Go over the report card with the students, answering any of their questions about how to complete it.
- Show the entire newscast.
- Replay, breaking the total news program into each news item:
  1. Show the first story of the newscast to the students.
  2. Stop the videotape.
  3. Discuss what they have seen so far.
  4. Would this story be classified as a positive or negative depiction?
  5. Repeat the process for each segment.
  6. Have the students assess the reporting of the stories overall.
  7. See if it changed from the initial grade that they gave.
  8. After the entire broadcast has been analyzed, have the students complete the report card.
  9. At the bottom of the page, have the students offer the station some advice on what they think the station could do to have a more inclusive and fair newscast for all communities.
  10. When all are done completing their report card, move to discussion questions:
      - How did you rate the newscast? Why?
      - What kinds of things did they do well?
      - What groups were well represented? How?
      - What groups were not well represented? How?
      - What advice did you give them to improve their newscast and make it both inclusive and fair to all?
      - How does this exercise change how you view the news? Does it give you a different idea of what the news is?
  11. A final activity is to invite a station representative to meet with the class.

FIELD STUDIES BY JAMES STECKART

Field studies offer my students "being there" experiences and are experiential education at its best. Nothing is more powerful and motivating than trips to an off-school site. Field studies bring the great ideas of books into our student's lives, with real and tangible experiences. It is one thing to study about the loss of habitat in the Florida Everglades, but it is another to be paddling a kayak your school built next to a pod of dolphins.

Field studies create lifelong learning moments. When asked, students remember the field study as one of the defining moments of their high school career. They are so powerful that I believe every student should have the opportunity to participate in one during his or her high school career. Some examples of field studies I have developed:

1. A water quality course with expeditions to the Florida Everglades, the Wind River Range in Wyoming, and the Mississippi and St. Croix Rivers.
2. Teaching a tolerance course on diversity, with an expedition to the Holocaust Museum in Washington, DC.
3. A rain-forest study course, with expeditions to Mt. Rainier, Olympic National Park, and Costa Rica.

Risk Management

When taking students away from the control and support of the school environment, we should realize the potential hazards of such activities. Special skills and judgment are needed by instructional staff to maintain the physical and emotional safety of students entrusted to our care. A conservative approach to planning activities and routes must be the mind-set. As a general guideline, staff who have not taken an expedition should be required to team with an experienced staff member before being the lead instructor for an expedition.

Qualifications of Instructors for Wilderness Context

1. One member of the instructional team must have the following certifications:

    a. Wilderness First Responder
    b. BLS CPR
    c. Lifeguard Training
2. One member of the instructional team must have documented experience in the type of wilderness activity students will be participating—for example, canoeing, kayaking, or backpacking.

Qualifications of Instructors for Urban Context

1. One member of the team needs to have basic first aid and CPR.
2. One member of the team must have documented experience leading extended expeditions in urban settings.

Planning Process

The following guidelines need to be considered before advertising the trip to students and their parents. All guidelines need to be approved by school administration and address school board policy.

1. Concept Review
    a. Learning objectives
    b. Site selection
    c. Budget
    d. Scholarship assistance
    e. Final project requirements for students
2. Scheduling

After approval, the following items need to be completed:

1. Flyer for Students
    a. Dates
    b. Times
    c. Cost
    d. Requirements
    e. Location
    f. Deposit (including the nonrefundable portion).
       If using air transportation, the deposit needs to be the amount for the flight. Note: No tickets can be purchased without the deposit.

2. Forms
   a. Permission slip (trip itself, medication, removal for discipline)
   b. Medical history form and medications
   c. Physical (needed if expedition is in a wilderness context)
3. Parent informational meeting; should be conducted well prior to the trip.
4. Emergency Action Plan
   a. List of hospitals in the area
   b. Phone numbers
   c. Agency contact information
   d. Detailed route plan and timeline

Equipment Use

Staff must use appropriate and approved equipment. The following guidelines need to be followed.

1. Checkout
   a. Schedule a checkout time with the equipment manager.
   b. Have students present for the checkout.
   c. Each student and staff taking personal equipment must fill out a checkout form.
   d. A group gear checkout list is required and staff is responsible for the group gear checked out.
3. Check-in
   a. All gear needs to be cleaned and checked.
   b. Schedule a check-in with the gear manager.
4. Vans
   a. Van drivers must meet requirements.
   b. Vans must meet requirements.
   c. Van need to be cleaned after the expedition.

Student Eligibility

Expeditions are special activities that enhance and enrich the school program. Our school believes that all students should participate in one trip prior to graduation. The following is a list of eligibility requirements for participation.

1. First priority of a trip shall go to students with the following:
   a. Students with fewer than eight credits remaining to graduate.
   b. Students who have a good attendance.
   c. Students who hold a job.
   d. Students who have never gone on an extended expedition.
   e. Students who demonstrate good behaviors while attending school.
2. Scholarships
   a. Student must demonstrate financial need based on free and reduced lunch eligibility.
   b. School will give a maximum of $200.
   c. A student may only receive one scholarship.

LOSERS TO WINNERS BY GARY PHILLIPS

The counselor at Rainier Beach High School in Seattle started a leadership class. She asked teachers to nominate one or two students from their classes who were difficult to work with. Teachers were happy to comply with the request.

She began by telling the students they had been selected for the class because their teachers saw leadership potential in them. The students beamed but wondered, as no one had told them this before.

She told them that during the next semester they were to become experts on some innovative school in America and that they would be making a presentation to the faculty about the information they had gathered. They would be traveling in pairs to a school selected from a list and would spend a week living with the family of students of that school. They would be doing interviews, taking photographs, shooting videos, and gathering as much information as possible. This was their assignment and the students were excited to be taking on such a challenge.

They then proceeded to make long lists of the skills and knowledge they would need in order to carry out the project in a competent manner.

Clearly, they would need to learn something about the schools and the community in order to make a wise choice. They were going to need to raise money, arrange travel, write letters, learn how to take notes, learn how to interview, and so on through a long and detailed list of items to master. Students practiced on each other using role-playing and obtaining feedback. They agreed that they wanted to do an excellent job to avoid making fools of themselves.

The students used a checklist of personal competencies as a record of their growing skills. One could see the students obtaining confidence and standing taller over the next several months. First, they practiced on half-day visits to local schools. As teams returned from local and distant visits, they reflected on the quality of the materials they collected and what went well and what could have been even better. Because the schools on the list were national models of innovation, students became excited about how their own school could be changed.

Before presentations to faculty, students polished their speaking techniques, prepared handouts, and made visual aids. They critiqued each other because they wanted to have a dramatic impact on their teachers.

Students made their presentations in a half-day faculty-staff development session. The teachers were amazed at the quality of the presentations and in addition were stretched in their thinking about how schools might be organized. They nominated the session as the best staff development they had received ever. In the view of the experts about these students, their former teachers, the students had gone from losers to winners in one semester.

REFERENCES

GENERAL

Aiken, W. (1942). *The story of the eight-year study*. New York: Harper and Brothers. (Note: This hugely important book is out of print but available on the web at www.8yearstudy.org/index.html.)

American Psychological Association. (1997). *Learner-centered psychological principles: A framework for school redesign and reform*. Washington, DC: Author.

Apple, M. W., & Beane, J. A. (Eds.). (1995). *Democratic schools*. Alexandria, VA: Association for Supervision and Curriculum Development.

Bloom, B. (1984). *Taxonomy of educational objectives, handbook 1: Cognitive domain*. Upper Saddle River, NJ: Addison-Wesley.

Caine, R., & Caine, G. (2001). *The brain, education and the competitive edge*. Lanham, MD: Rowman & Littlefield.

Caulfield, J., & Jennings, W. (2002). *Inciting learning: A guide to brain-compatible instruction*. Reston, VA: National Association of Secondary School Principals.

Chugani, H. T. (1999). Basic mechansims of childhood epilepsies: Studies with positron emission tomography. *Advances in Neurology, 79*, 883–891.

Csikszentmihalyi, M. (1993). *Flow: The psychology of optimal experience*. London: HarperCollins.

Damasio, A. (1994). *Descartes' error: Emotion, reason, and the human brain*. New York: G. P. Putnam's Sons.

De Bono, E. (1999). *Six thinking hats.* Boston: Little, Brown.

Della Neve, C., et al. (1986, October). Huge learning jumps show potency of brain-based instruction. *Phi Delta Kappan, 68*(2): 143–148.

Diamond, M. (1988). *Enriching heredity: The impact of the environment on the anatomy of the brain.* New York: Free Press.

Diamond, M., Hopson, J. L., & Diamond, M. C. (1998). *Magic trees of the mind: How to nurture your child's intelligence, creativity, and healthy emotions from birth through adolescence.* New York: Dutton.

Dunn, R. S., & Dunn, K. J. (1993). *Teaching secondary students through their individual learning styles: Practical approaches for grades 7–12.* Upper Saddle River, NJ: Pearson Education.

Dunston, P. J. (1992) A critique of graphic organizer research. *Reading Research and Instruction, 31*(2), 57–65.

Fogarty, R. (2002). *Brain-compatible classrooms* (2nd ed.). Arlington Heights, IL: Skylight Professional Development.

Gardner, H. (1983). *Frames of mind: The theory of multiple intelligences.* New York: Basic Books.

Gloman, C. B. (2003). *303 digital filmmaking solutions: Solve any video shoot or edit problem in ten minutes or less, for ten dollars or less.* New York: McGraw Hill.

Goleman, D. (1995). *Emotional intelligence: Why it can matter more than IQ.* New York: Bantam Books.

Gould, E. J., & Gould, J. S. (2002). *Four square: The total writing classroom for grades 5–9.* Carthage, IL: Teaching & Learning.

Gregorc, A. F. (1985). *Inside styles: Beyond the basics.* Maynard, MA: Gabriel Systems.

Gregory, G., & Chapman, C. (2001). *Differentiated instructional strategies: One size doesn't fit all.* Thousand Oaks, CA: Corwin Press.

Hansel, B. (1993). *The exchange student survival kit.* Yarmouth, ME: Intercultural Press.

Hart, L. A. (1993). *Anchor math: The brain-compatible approach to learning.* Covington, WA: Books for Educators.

Hart, L. A. (1998). *Human brain and human learning.* Kent, WA: Books for Educators.

Jennings, W. (Ed.). (1995). *Community learning centers.* St. Paul, MN: Designs for Learning.

Jensen, E. (1998). *Teaching with the brain in mind.* Alexandria, VA: Association for Supervision and Curriculum Development.

Kagan, S., & Rodriguez, C. (1997). *Cooperative learning.* San Clemente, CA: Kagan Cooperative Learning.

Kaye, C. B. (2003). *The complete guide to service learning: Proven, practical ways to engage students in civic responsibility, academic curriculum, and social action*. Minneapolis, MN: Free Spirit Publishing.

Kovalik, S., & Olsen, K. (1994). *Integrated thematic instruction: The model* (3rd ed.). Covington, WA: Books for Educators.

Kovalik, S., & Olsen, K. (2001). *Exceeding expectations: A user's guide to implementing brain research in the classroom*. Covington, WA: Books for Educators.

Krishnaswami, U. (2002). *Beyond the field trip: Teaching and learning in public places*. North Haven, CT: Shoe String Press.

LeDoux, J. (1996). *The emotional brain: The mysterious underpinning of emotional life*. New York: Simon & Schuster.

Linde, B. M. (1996). *The light in the forest: A unit plan*. Berlin, MD: Teacher's Pet Publications.

Lisle, D. (2001). *Imaging for students*. London: Edward Arnold.

Mandell, J., & Wolf, J. L. (2003). *Acting, learning, and change: Creating original plays with adolescents*. Portsmouth, NH: Heinemann.

McCarthy, B. (2000). *4Mat about teaching; Format in the classroom*. Barrington, IL: Excel.

National Association of Secondary School Principals. (2004). *Breaking ranks II: Strategies for leading high school reform*. Reston, VA: National Association of Secondary School Principals.

National Institute of Mental Health. (2001). *Teenage brain: A work in progress*. Bethesda, MD: Author.

National Research Council. (2000). *How people learn: Brain, mind, experience, and school*. Washington, DC: National Academy Press.

Newell, R. J. (2003). *Passion for learning: How project-based learning meets the needs of 21st century students*. Lanham, MD: Rowman & Littlefield.

Pert, C. (1997). *Molecules of emotion*. New York: Scribner.

Phelps, M. (2003). *PET: Molecular imaging and its biological applications*. New York: Springer-Verlag.

Public Education Network. (2003, August 15). *Weekly Newsblast* [Television broadcast].

Ramey, C. T., & Ramey, S. L. (1999). *Right from birth: Building your child's foundation for life*. New York: Goddard Press.

Richter, C. (1953). *The light in the forest*. New York: Knopf.

Smith, F. (1988). *Insult to intelligence: The bureaucratic invasion of our classrooms*. Portsmouth, NH: Heinemann.

Spolin, V. (1986). *Theater games for the classroom: A teacher's handbook*. Evanston, IL: Northwestern University Press.

Styles, D. (2001). *Class meetings: Building leadership, problem-solving and decision-making skills in the respectful classroom*. Markham, Canada: Pembroke.

Temple, E., et al. (2003, March) Neural deficits in children with dyslexia ameliorated by behavioral remediation: Evidence from functional MRI. *Proceedings of the National Academy of Sciences of the USA*, 100 (pp. 2860-2865).

Thiagarajan, S. (2003). *Design your own games and activities: Thiagi's templates for performance improvement*. San Francisco: Jossey-Bass/Pfeiffer.

Tomlinson, C. A. (2003). *Differentiation in practice: A resource guide for differentiating curriculum, grades 5–9*. Alexandria, VA: Association for Supervision and Curriculum Development.

Wolfe, P. (2001). *Brain matters: Translating research into classroom practice*. Alexandria, VA: Association for Supervision and Curriculum Development.

FURTHER READING

Ackerman, S. (1992). *Discovering the brain*. Washington, DC: National Academy Press.

Amaral, D., & Soltesz, I. (1997). *Encyclopedia of human biology* (2nd ed., Vol. 4). New York: Academic Press.

Armstrong, T. (1994). *Multiple intelligences in the classroom*. Alexandria, VA: Association for Supervision and Curriculum Development.

Armstrong, T. (1997). *Awakening genius in the classroom*. Alexandria, VA: Association for Supervision and Curriculum Development.

Armstrong, T. (1999). *7 kinds of smart: Identifying and developing your multiple intelligences*. New York: Plume.

Armstrong, T. (2000). *In their own way: Discovering and encouraging your child's multiple intelligences*. Los Angeles: J. P. Tarcher.

Balog, D. (Ed.). (2003). *The Dana sourcebook of brain science*. New York: Dana Press.

Bear, M. F., Conners, B. W., & Paraqdiso, M. A. (1996). *Neuroscience: Exploring the brain*. New York: Lippincott.

Biller, L. W. (2003). *Creating brain-friendly classrooms*. Lanham, MD: Scarecrow Press.

Binney, R., & Jason, M. (1990). *Atlas of the mind and body*. London: Mitchell Beazley.

Brandt, R. (1998). *Powerful learning*. Alexandria, VA: Association for Supervision and Curriculum Development.

Bruer, J. T. (1994). *Schools for thought: A science of learning in the classroom.* Cambridge, MA: MIT Press.

Bruer, J. T. (1999, May). In search of brain-based education. *Phi Delta Kappan, 80*(9): 648–654, 656–657.

Caine, G., et al. (1999). *Mindshifts* (2nd ed.). Tucson, AZ: Zephyr Press.

Caine, R., & Caine, G. (1991). *Making connections: Teaching and the human brain.* Alexandria, VA: Association for Supervision and Curriculum Development.

Caine, R., & Caine, G. (1997). *Education on the edge of possibility.* Alexandria, VA: Association for Supervision and Curriculum Development.

Caine, R., et al. (1997). *Unleashing the power of perceptual change: The potential of brain-based teaching.* Alexandria, VA: Association for Supervision and Curriculum Development.

Calvin, W. H. (1996). *How brains think: Evolving intelligence then and now.* New York: Basic Books.

Carter, R. (1998). *Mapping the mind.* Los Angeles: University of California Press.

Countryman, J. (1992). *Writing to learn mathematics: Strategies that work, K–12.* Portsmouth, NH: Heinemann.

Crick, F. (1994). *The astonishing hypothesis: The scientific search for the soul.* New York: Scribners.

Crowel, S., et al. (1997). *The re-enchantment of learning.* Tucson, AZ: Zephyr Press.

Davis, J. (1997). *Mapping the mind: The secrets of the human brain and how it works.* Secaucus, NJ: Birch Lane Press.

Delisle, R. (1997). *How to use problem-based learning in the classroom.* Alexandria, VA: Association for Supervision and Curriculum Development.

Dennison, P., & Dennison, G. (1994). *Brain gym.* Ventura, CA: Edu-Kinesthetics.

Drubach, D. (1999). *The brain explained.* Upper Saddle River, NJ: Prentice-Hall.

Elias, M. J., et al. (1997). *Promoting social and emotional learning.* Alexandria, VA: Association for Supervision and Curriculum Development.

Ellison, L. (1993). *Seeing with magic glasses: A teacher's view from the front line of the learning revolution.* Arlington, VA: Great Ocean Publishers.

Ellison, L. (2000). *The personal intelligences: Promoting social and emotional learning.* Thousand Oaks, CA: Corwin Press.

Erlauer, L. (2003). *The brain-compatible classroom: Using what we know about learning to improve instruction.* Alexandria, VA: Association for Supervision and Curriculum Development.

Forestor, A., Reinhard, M., & Caine, R. (2000). *The learners' way: Brain-based learning in action*: Winnipeg, Canada: Peguis.

Gazzaniga, M. (1997). *Conversations in the neurosciences*. Cambridge, MA: MIT Press.

Gazzaniga, M. (1998). *The mind's past*. Berkeley: University of California Press.

Gazzaniga, M., Ivry, R., & Mangun, R. (1998). *Cognitive neuroscience*. New York: W. W. Norton.

Givens, B. (2002). *Teaching to the brain's natural learning systems*. Alexandria, VA: Association for Supervision and Curriculum Development.

Glines, D. (2002). *Educational alternatives for everyone: A handbook for educators, families, politicians*. St. Paul, MN: International Association for Learning Alternatives.

Grandin, T. (1995). *Thinking in pictures*. New York: Doubleday.

Greenfield, S. (1996). *The human mind examined*. New York: Henry Holt.

Greenfield, S. (1997). *The human brain: A guided tour*. New York: Basic Books.

Greenspan, S., et al. (1997). *The growth of the mind and the endangered origins of intelligence*. Reading, MA: Addison-Wesley.

Gregory, R. (Ed.). (1987). *The Oxford companion to the mind*. New York: Oxford University Press.

Gurian, M., et al. (2001). *Boys and girls learn differently! A guide for teachers and parents*. San Francisco: Jossey-Bass.

Handy, C. B. (1998). *The hungry spirit*. New York: Broadway Books.

Harth, E. (1993). *The creative loop: How the brain makes a mind*. Reading, MA: Addison-Wesley.

Healy, J. (1990). *Endangered minds: Why our children don't think*. New York: Touchstone.

Healy, J. (1994). *Your child's growing mind: A guide to learning and brain development from birth to adolescence*. Honesdale, PA: Main St. Books.

Hilt, P. J. (1995). *Memory's ghost*. New York: Simon & Schuster.

Hobson, J. A. (1989). *Sleep*. New York: Scientific American Library.

Hooper, J., & Teresi, D. (1986). *The 3-pound universe*. New York: Dell.

Howard, P. (2000). *The owner's manual for the brain: Everyday applications from mind-brain research*. Austin, TX: Bard Press.

Hyerle, D. (1996). *Visual tools for constructing knowledge*. Alexandria, VA: Association for Supervision and Curriculum Development.

Hyerle, D. (2000). *A field guide to using visual tools*. Alexandria, VA: Association for Supervision and Curriculum Development.

Jensen, E. (1995a). *Brain-based learning and teaching*. San Diego: Brain Store.

Jensen, E. (1995b). *The learning brain*. San Diego: Brain Store.

Jensen, E. (1996). *Completing the puzzle: The brain-based approach.* San Diego: Brain Store.

Jensen, E. (1998). *Introduction to brain compatible learning.* San Diego: Brain Store.

Jensen, E. (2000a). *Learning with the body in mind.* San Diego: Brain Store.

Jensen, E. (2000b). *Music with the brain in mind.* San Diego: Brain Store.

Jensen, E. (2001). *Arts with the brain in mind.* Alexandria, VA: Association for Supervision and Curriculum Development.

Joyce, B., & Showers, B. (1988). *Student achievement through staff development.* New York: Longman.

Kaufeldt, M. (1999). *Begin with the brain: Orchestrating the learner centered classroom.* Tucson, AZ: Zephyr Press.

Kotulak, R. (1997). *Inside the brain: Revolutionary discoveries of how the mind works.* Kansas City, MO: Andrews & McMeel.

Lambert, M. N., & McCombs, B. L. (1998). *How students learn: Reforming schools through learner-centered education.* Washington, DC: American Psychological Association.

Lazear, D. G. (1998). *Eight ways of knowing.* Arlington Heights, IL: Skylight Professional Development.

Levinthal, C. F. (1988). *Messengers in paradise: Opiates and the brain.* New York: Anchor Press/Doubleday.

Margulies, N. (1996). *Inside Brian's brain* [comic book]. Tucson, AZ: Zephyr Press.

Morowitz, H., et al. (1995). *The mind, the brain and complex adaptive systems.* Reading, MA: Santa Fe Institute, Addison-Wesley.

Moyers, B. (1993). *Healing and the mind.* New York: Doubleday.

Noah, G. F. (1995). *Magical classroom: Creating effective, brain-friendly environments for learning.* Tucson, AZ: Zephyr Press.

November, A. (2001). *Empowering students with technology.* Glenview, IL: Pearson Professional Development.

Olsen, K. (1996). *Science continuum of concepts for grades K–6.* Covington, WA: Books for Educators.

Olsen, K., & Kovalik, S. (1999). *ITI classroom stages of implementation.* Covington, WA: Books for Educators.

Ornstein, R. (1991). *The evolution of consciousness: The origins of the way we think.* New York: Simon & Schuster.

Ornstein, R. (1997). *The right mind.* Orlando, FL: Harcourt Brace.

Ornstein, R. (1998). *Psychology: The study of human experience* (2nd ed.). San Diego: Harcourt Brace Jovanovich.

Ornstein, R., & Sobel, D. S. (1999). *The healing brain.* New York: Malor Books.

Parry, T., et al. (2003). *Designing brain compatible learning*. Arlington Heights, IL: Skylight Professional Development.

Perkins, D. (1992). *Smart schools: From training memories to educating minds*. New York: Free Press.

Perkins, D. (1995). *Outsmarting I.Q.: The emerging science of learnable intelligence*. New York: Free Press.

Pinker, S. (1999). *How the mind works*. New York: W. W. Norton.

Pinker, S. (2000). *The language instinct: The new science of the language and the mind*. New York: Harper Perennial Library.

Posner, M. I., & Raichle, M. E. (1997). *Images of mind*. New York: W. H. Freeman.

Ratey, J. (2001). *A user's guide to the brain*. New York: Pantheon Books.

Restak, R. (1994). *Receptors*. New York: Bantam Books.

Restak, R. (2000). *Mysteries of the mind*. Washington, DC: National Geographic Society.

Restak, R. (2001a). *Mozart's brain and the fighter pilot*. New York: Harmony Books.

Restak, R. (2001b). *The secret life of the brain*. Washington, DC: Joseph Henry Press.

Robinson, F. P. (1970). *Effective study*. New York: HarperCollins.

Sapolsky, R. (1994). *Why zebras don't get ulcers*. New York: W. H. Freeman.

Schacter, D. (1996). *Searching for memory, the brain, the mind, and the past*. New York: Basic Books.

Shaw, G. (2000). *Keeping Mozart in mind*. San Diego: Academic Press.

Siegel, D. J. (1999). *The developing mind: Toward a neurobiology of interpersonal experience*. New York: Guilford Press.

Sousa, D. (2000). *How the brain learns*. Thousand Oaks, CA: Corwin Press.

Springer, M. (1999). *Learning and memory: The brain in action*. Alexandria, VA: Association for Supervision and Curriculum Development.

Springer, M. (2001). *Becoming a "wiz" at brain-based teaching: From translation to application*. Thousand Oaks, CA: Corwin Press.

Squire, L. R., & Kandel, E. R. (2000). *Memory from mind to molecules*. New York: Scientific American Library.

Sternberg, R. J. (2000). *Handbook of intelligence*. Cambridge: Cambridge University Press.

Sylwester, R. (1995). *A celebration of neurons: An educator's guide to the human brain*. Alexandria, VA: Association for Supervision and Curriculum Development.

Sylwester, R. (1998). *Student brains, school issues: A collection of articles*. Glenview, IL: Skylight Professional Development.

Sylwester, R. (2000). *Brain-compatible strategies*. Thousand Oaks, CA: Corwin Press.

Teachers' Curriculum Institute. (1999). *History alive! Engaging all learners in the diverse classroom*. Mountain View, CA: Teachers' Curriculum Institute.

Thompson, R. (1985). *The brain: An introduction to neuroscience*. New York: W. H. Freeman.

Torp, L., & Sage, S. (1998). *Problems as possibilities: Problem-based learning for K–12 education*. Alexandria, VA: Association for Supervision and Curriculum Development.

Van Der Meer, R., et al. (1996). *The brain pack: A 3-dimensional exploration of the mysteries of the mind*. Philadelphia: Running Press.

INDEX

active learning, 19
advisor–advisee program, 70
advisory program, 17, 21
American Psychological Association, ix
assessment: peer, 20; self, 20
Association for Experiential Education, 66

Bloom's Taxonomy, 37, 41, 44, 47, 107
brain: abilities, 5; amygdala, 4, 8; applications for learning, 3–4; compatible learning, 16; connections, 12–13; facts, 24; feedback, 14, 19–20, 22; growth, 5–6; imaging, 1–3; meaning 11–12; neurons, 4; not fixed, 6; research, 4; security, 8; stimulation, 9–10
brain-compatible learning, 16; feedback, 14, 19–20, 22; input, 18;

meaningful learning, 18–19; rich, stimulating environment, 18; safe, secure setting, 17
Breaking Ranks II, 21

Caine, Geoffery, 3–4
Caine, Renate, 3–4
Caulfield, Joan, 4
celebrations, 20
chalk talks, 34–36
choice, 11; boards, 41–43
Chugani, Harry, 3, 5
class meetings, 77–79
coaching, 20
committees and task forces, 66–68
Community Learning Centers, 68
community service, 74–75
conferences, 20
cooperative learning, 20
Cooperative Learning, 68
Csikszentmihalyi, Mihaly, 3
cubing, 44–48

ABOUT THE AUTHORS

Wayne Jennings is a former teacher, principal, superintendent, and adjunct professor and has started eight schools during his career in education. He is coauthor of *Inciting Learning: A Guide to Brain-Compatible Learning* and cofacilitator of the ASCD Brain-Compatible Learning Network.

Joan Caulfield is a former teacher, principal, associate superintendent, and professor of education and is currently a nationally known staff developer and consultant in teaching and learning. She is coauthor of *Inciting Learning: A Guide to Brain-Compatible Learning* and cofacilitator of the ASCD Brain-Compatible Learning Network.